GARDEN
PLANNER

This Planner Belongs To:

_____

Planner Timeline:

_____

HARDINESS ZONE: _____

SOIL TYPE & Ph: _____

LAST SPRING FROST: _____

FIRST FALL FROST: _____

REVIVE *stationery*

Garden Planner

ISBN: 978-1-83412-085-0

TIP

THIS PLANNER OFTEN HAS A NUMBERING (#) SPOT AVAILABLE.

USE THESE TO NUMBER AND LINK THE SUPPLIERS OR PLANTS

FROM YOUR INVENTORIES TO OTHER LISTS FOR REFERENCE.

GARDEN WISH LIST

FAVORITE SUPPLIERS

 # S _____ ☐ ONLINE ☐ IN PERSON   RATING ☆☆☆☆☆

NAME

ADDRESS

PURCHASE RATE RARELY / SEASONALLY / REGULARLY

NOTES

 # S _____ ☐ ONLINE ☐ IN PERSON   RATING ☆☆☆☆☆

NAME

ADDRESS

PURCHASE RATE RARELY / SEASONALLY / REGULARLY

NOTES

 # S _____ ☐ ONLINE ☐ IN PERSON   RATING ☆☆☆☆☆

NAME

ADDRESS

PURCHASE RATE RARELY / SEASONALLY / REGULARLY

NOTES

 # S _____ ☐ ONLINE ☐ IN PERSON   RATING ☆☆☆☆☆

NAME

ADDRESS

PURCHASE RATE RARELY / SEASONALLY / REGULARLY

NOTES

 # S _____ ☐ ONLINE ☐ IN PERSON   RATING ☆☆☆☆☆

NAME

ADDRESS

PURCHASE RATE RARELY / SEASONALLY / REGULARLY

NOTES

 # S _____ ☐ ONLINE ☐ IN PERSON   RATING ☆☆☆☆☆

NAME

ADDRESS

PURCHASE RATE RARELY / SEASONALLY / REGULARLY

NOTES

 # S _____ ☐ ONLINE ☐ IN PERSON   RATING ☆☆☆☆☆

NAME

ADDRESS

PURCHASE RATE RARELY / SEASONALLY / REGULARLY

NOTES

 # S _____ ☐ ONLINE ☐ IN PERSON   RATING ☆☆☆☆☆

NAME

ADDRESS

PURCHASE RATE RARELY / SEASONALLY / REGULARLY

NOTES

FAVORITE SUPPLIERS

S _____ ☐ ONLINE ☐ IN PERSON RATING ☆☆☆☆☆

NAME

ADDRESS

PURCHASE RATE RARELY / SEASONALLY / REGULARLY

NOTES

S _____ ☐ ONLINE ☐ IN PERSON RATING ☆☆☆☆☆

NAME

ADDRESS

PURCHASE RATE RARELY / SEASONALLY / REGULARLY

NOTES

S _____ ☐ ONLINE ☐ IN PERSON RATING ☆☆☆☆☆

NAME

ADDRESS

PURCHASE RATE RARELY / SEASONALLY / REGULARLY

NOTES

S _____ ☐ ONLINE ☐ IN PERSON RATING ☆☆☆☆☆

NAME

ADDRESS

PURCHASE RATE RARELY / SEASONALLY / REGULARLY

NOTES

S _____ ☐ ONLINE ☐ IN PERSON RATING ☆☆☆☆☆

NAME

ADDRESS

PURCHASE RATE RARELY / SEASONALLY / REGULARLY

NOTES

S _____ ☐ ONLINE ☐ IN PERSON RATING ☆☆☆☆☆

NAME

ADDRESS

PURCHASE RATE RARELY / SEASONALLY / REGULARLY

NOTES

S _____ ☐ ONLINE ☐ IN PERSON RATING ☆☆☆☆☆

NAME

ADDRESS

PURCHASE RATE RARELY / SEASONALLY / REGULARLY

NOTES

S _____ ☐ ONLINE ☐ IN PERSON RATING ☆☆☆☆☆

NAME

ADDRESS

PURCHASE RATE RARELY / SEASONALLY / REGULARLY

NOTES

MONTH AT A GLANCE

JANUARY

SUNDAY	MONDAY	TUESDAY	WEDNESDAY	THURSDAY	FRIDAY	SATURDAY

TO-DO LIST

MONTH AT A GLANCE

FEBRUARY						
SUNDAY	MONDAY	TUESDAY	WEDNESDAY	THURSDAY	FRIDAY	SATURDAY

TO-DO LIST

MONTH AT A GLANCE

MARCH

SUNDAY	MONDAY	TUESDAY	WEDNESDAY	THURSDAY	FRIDAY	SATURDAY

TO-DO LIST

MONTH AT A GLANCE

APRIL

SUNDAY	MONDAY	TUESDAY	WEDNESDAY	THURSDAY	FRIDAY	SATURDAY

TO-DO LIST

MONTH AT A GLANCE

MAY						
SUNDAY	MONDAY	TUESDAY	WEDNESDAY	THURSDAY	FRIDAY	SATURDAY

TO-DO LIST

MONTH AT A GLANCE

JUNE

SUNDAY	MONDAY	TUESDAY	WEDNESDAY	THURSDAY	FRIDAY	SATURDAY

TO-DO LIST

MONTH AT A GLANCE

JULY						
SUNDAY	MONDAY	TUESDAY	WEDNESDAY	THURSDAY	FRIDAY	SATURDAY

18

TO-DO LIST

MONTH AT A GLANCE

AUGUST						
SUNDAY	MONDAY	TUESDAY	WEDNESDAY	THURSDAY	FRIDAY	SATURDAY

TO-DO LIST

MONTH AT A GLANCE

SEPTEMBER

SUNDAY	MONDAY	TUESDAY	WEDNESDAY	THURSDAY	FRIDAY	SATURDAY

TO-DO LIST

MONTH AT A GLANCE

OCTOBER						
SUNDAY	MONDAY	TUESDAY	WEDNESDAY	THURSDAY	FRIDAY	SATURDAY

TO-DO LIST

MONTH AT A GLANCE

NOVEMBER

SUNDAY	MONDAY	TUESDAY	WEDNESDAY	THURSDAY	FRIDAY	SATURDAY

TO-DO LIST

MONTH AT A GLANCE

DECEMBER						
SUNDAY	MONDAY	TUESDAY	WEDNESDAY	THURSDAY	FRIDAY	SATURDAY

TO-DO LIST

GARDEN LAYOUT

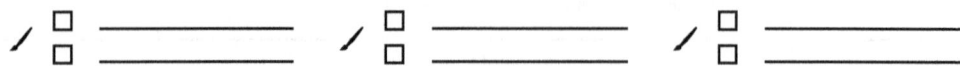

/ ☐☐ ———————   / ☐☐ ———————   / ☐☐ ———————

GARDEN DESCRIPTION

AREA NAME _____

PURPOSE _____

_____

TREATMENTS _____

_____

SUN EXPOSURE ☼ ☐ ◐ ☐ ● ☐

HOURS OF SUN ____ ☐ AM ☐ PM ☐

WATERING NEEDS _____

PRUNING NEEDS RARELY / SEASONALLY / REGULARLY

SOIL AMENDMENTS _____

#	✓	PLANT LIST	QTY	🌱	💧
	☐			☐	☐
	☐			☐	☐
	☐			☐	☐
	☐			☐	☐
	☐			☐	☐
	☐			☐	☐
	☐			☐	☐
	☐			☐	☐
	☐			☐	☐
	☐			☐	☐

NOTES _____

_____

_____

_____

_____

_____

_____

_____

_____

GARDEN LAYOUT

GARDEN DESCRIPTION

AREA NAME _____

PURPOSE _____

_____

TREATMENTS _____

_____

SUN EXPOSURE ☼ ☐ ☀ ☐ ☀ ☐
                     ☐ AM ☐ PM

HOURS OF SUN _____ ☐

WATERING NEEDS _____

PRUNING NEEDS   RARELY / SEASONALLY / REGULARLY

SOIL AMENDMENTS _____

#	✓	PLANT LIST	QTY	🌱	💧
	☐			☐	☐
	☐			☐	☐
	☐			☐	☐
	☐			☐	☐
	☐			☐	☐
	☐			☐	☐
	☐			☐	☐
	☐			☐	☐
	☐			☐	☐
	☐			☐	☐

NOTES

_____

_____

_____

_____

_____

_____

_____

_____

GARDEN LAYOUT

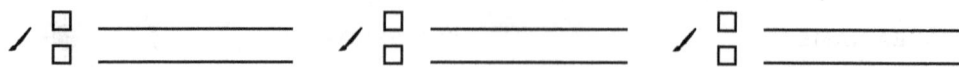

/ ▫▫ ═══════   / ▫▫ ═══════   / ▫▫ ═══════

GARDEN DESCRIPTION

AREA NAME _____

PURPOSE _____

_____

TREATMENTS _____

_____

SUN EXPOSURE ☼ ☐ ☀ ☐ ☀ ☐

☐ AM   ☐ PM

HOURS OF SUN ☐

WATERING NEEDS _____

PRUNING NEEDS   RARELY / SEASONALLY / REGULARLY

SOIL AMENDMENTS _____

#	✓	PLANT LIST	QTY	🌱	💧
	☐			☐	☐
	☐			☐	☐
	☐			☐	☐
	☐			☐	☐
	☐			☐	☐
	☐			☐	☐
	☐			☐	☐
	☐			☐	☐
	☐			☐	☐
	☐			☐	☐

NOTES

_____

_____

_____

_____

_____

_____

_____

_____

_____

GARDEN LAYOUT

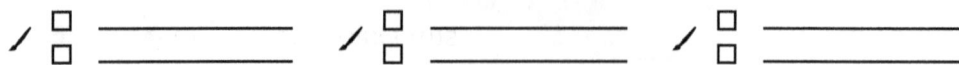

/ □□ ———— ———— / □□ ———— ———— / □□ ————

GARDEN DESCRIPTION

AREA NAME _____

PURPOSE _____

_____

TREATMENTS _____

_____

SUN EXPOSURE ☼ ☐ 🌓 ☐ ☀ ☐

HOURS OF SUN ☐ AM   ☐ PM
_____ ☐

WATERING NEEDS _____

PRUNING NEEDS   RARELY / SEASONALLY / REGULARLY

SOIL AMENDMENTS _____

#	✓	PLANT LIST	QTY	🌿	💧
	☐			☐	☐
	☐			☐	☐
	☐			☐	☐
	☐			☐	☐
	☐			☐	☐
	☐			☐	☐
	☐			☐	☐
	☐			☐	☐
	☐			☐	☐
	☐			☐	☐

NOTES

_____

_____

_____

_____

_____

_____

_____

_____

_____

GARDEN LAYOUT

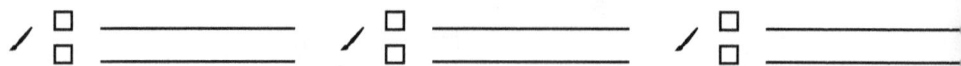

GARDEN DESCRIPTION

AREA NAME

PURPOSE

TREATMENTS

SUN EXPOSURE ☼ ☐ ◑ ☐ ● ☐

HOURS OF SUN ☐ AM ☐ PM
☐

WATERING NEEDS

PRUNING NEEDS RARELY / SEASONALLY / REGULARLY

SOIL AMENDMENTS

#	✓	PLANT LIST	QTY	🌱	💧
	☐			☐	☐
	☐			☐	☐
	☐			☐	☐
	☐			☐	☐
	☐			☐	☐
	☐			☐	☐
	☐			☐	☐
	☐			☐	☐
	☐			☐	☐
	☐			☐	☐

NOTES

PLANT INVENTORY
KEEP TRACK OF YOUR PLANTS IN ONE PLACE!

#	PLANT NAME	GARDEN	QTY	NEW?	RATING
				☐	☆☆☆☆☆
				☐	☆☆☆☆☆
				☐	☆☆☆☆☆
				☐	☆☆☆☆☆
				☐	☆☆☆☆☆
				☐	☆☆☆☆☆
				☐	☆☆☆☆☆
				☐	☆☆☆☆☆
				☐	☆☆☆☆☆
				☐	☆☆☆☆☆
				☐	☆☆☆☆☆
				☐	☆☆☆☆☆
				☐	☆☆☆☆☆
				☐	☆☆☆☆☆
				☐	☆☆☆☆☆
				☐	☆☆☆☆☆
				☐	☆☆☆☆☆
				☐	☆☆☆☆☆
				☐	☆☆☆☆☆
				☐	☆☆☆☆☆
				☐	☆☆☆☆☆
				☐	☆☆☆☆☆
				☐	☆☆☆☆☆
				☐	☆☆☆☆☆
				☐	☆☆☆☆☆
				☐	☆☆☆☆☆

PLANT INVENTORY
KEEP TRACK OF YOUR PLANTS IN ONE PLACE!

#	PLANT NAME	GARDEN	QTY	NEW?	RATING
				☐	☆☆☆☆☆
				☐	☆☆☆☆☆
				☐	☆☆☆☆☆
				☐	☆☆☆☆☆
				☐	☆☆☆☆☆
				☐	☆☆☆☆☆
				☐	☆☆☆☆☆
				☐	☆☆☆☆☆
				☐	☆☆☆☆☆
				☐	☆☆☆☆☆
				☐	☆☆☆☆☆
				☐	☆☆☆☆☆
				☐	☆☆☆☆☆
				☐	☆☆☆☆☆
				☐	☆☆☆☆☆
				☐	☆☆☆☆☆
				☐	☆☆☆☆☆
				☐	☆☆☆☆☆
				☐	☆☆☆☆☆
				☐	☆☆☆☆☆
				☐	☆☆☆☆☆
				☐	☆☆☆☆☆
				☐	☆☆☆☆☆
				☐	☆☆☆☆☆
				☐	☆☆☆☆☆

PLANT INVENTORY

KEEP TRACK OF YOUR PLANTS IN ONE PLACE!

#	PLANT NAME	GARDEN	QTY	NEW?	RATING
				☐	☆☆☆☆☆
				☐	☆☆☆☆☆
				☐	☆☆☆☆☆
				☐	☆☆☆☆☆
				☐	☆☆☆☆☆
				☐	☆☆☆☆☆
				☐	☆☆☆☆☆
				☐	☆☆☆☆☆
				☐	☆☆☆☆☆
				☐	☆☆☆☆☆
				☐	☆☆☆☆☆
				☐	☆☆☆☆☆
				☐	☆☆☆☆☆
				☐	☆☆☆☆☆
				☐	☆☆☆☆☆
				☐	☆☆☆☆☆
				☐	☆☆☆☆☆
				☐	☆☆☆☆☆
				☐	☆☆☆☆☆
				☐	☆☆☆☆☆
				☐	☆☆☆☆☆
				☐	☆☆☆☆☆
				☐	☆☆☆☆☆
				☐	☆☆☆☆☆
				☐	☆☆☆☆☆

PLANT INVENTORY
KEEP TRACK OF YOUR PLANTS IN ONE PLACE!

#	PLANT NAME	GARDEN	QTY	NEW?	RATING
				☐	☆☆☆☆☆
				☐	☆☆☆☆☆
				☐	☆☆☆☆☆
				☐	☆☆☆☆☆
				☐	☆☆☆☆☆
				☐	☆☆☆☆☆
				☐	☆☆☆☆☆
				☐	☆☆☆☆☆
				☐	☆☆☆☆☆
				☐	☆☆☆☆☆
				☐	☆☆☆☆☆
				☐	☆☆☆☆☆
				☐	☆☆☆☆☆
				☐	☆☆☆☆☆
				☐	☆☆☆☆☆
				☐	☆☆☆☆☆
				☐	☆☆☆☆☆
				☐	☆☆☆☆☆
				☐	☆☆☆☆☆
				☐	☆☆☆☆☆
				☐	☆☆☆☆☆
				☐	☆☆☆☆☆
				☐	☆☆☆☆☆
				☐	☆☆☆☆☆
				☐	☆☆☆☆☆

SEED TRACKER

COLOR THE STORY OF YOUR GARDEN LIFE CYCLE!

/ ☐ SOWN   / ☐ SPROUTED   / ☐ _____
/ ☐ GERMINATED   ☐ BLOOMED/HARVESTED   ☐ _____

#	PLANT	J	F	M	A	M	J	J	A	S	O	N	D

SEED TRACKER

COLOR THE STORY OF YOUR GARDEN LIFE CYCLE!

☐ SOWN   ☐ SPROUTED   ☐ _____
☐ GERMINATED   ☐ BLOOMED/HARVESTED   ☐ _____

#	PLANT	J	F	M	A	M	J	J	A	S	O	N	D

TREATMENT TRACKER

COLOR CODE YOUR TREATMENTS FOR EASY TRACKING!

/ ☐ FERTILIZER   / ☐ DISEASE PREVENTION/CURE   / ☐ _____
  ☐ PEST CONTROL   ☐ _____   ☐ _____

#S	#	NAME	J	F	M	A	M	J	J	A	S	O	N	D

TREATMENT TRACKER
REFLECT ON THE TREATMENT

FAVORITES

RESULTS	RATING
	☆☆☆☆☆
	☆☆☆☆☆
	☆☆☆☆☆
	☆☆☆☆☆
	☆☆☆☆☆
	☆☆☆☆☆
	☆☆☆☆☆
	☆☆☆☆☆
	☆☆☆☆☆
	☆☆☆☆☆
	☆☆☆☆☆
	☆☆☆☆☆
	☆☆☆☆☆
	☆☆☆☆☆
	☆☆☆☆☆
	☆☆☆☆☆
	☆☆☆☆☆
	☆☆☆☆☆
	☆☆☆☆☆

PLANT DESCRIPTION

#_____ **NAME** _____ **SUPPLIER** _____ **PRICE** _____
#S

LIGHT REQUIREMENTS	WATERING REQUIREMENTS	ZONE HARDINESS	NEED TO OVERWINTER?
☼ ☐ ☀ ☐ ● ☐	◊ ◊◊ ◊◊◊	_____	☐ YES ☐ NO DATE

NEW-TO-ME PLANT? **QTY** **TYPE** ☐ FLOWER ☐ FRUIT ☐ VEGETABLE ☐ HERB
☐ YES ☐ NO _____ ☐ SHRUB ☐ TREE ☐ OTHER: _____

LIFE CYCLE ☐ ANNUAL ☐ BIENNIAL ☐ PERENNIAL

GARDEN LOCATION(S)
_____
_____

MATURE SIZE
_____ _____
HEIGHT WIDTH

PRUNING REQUIRED?
☐ YES   ☐ NO

PRUNING RATE
RARELY / SEASONALLY / REGULARLY

PESTS
☐ YES   ☐ NO

TREATMENT USED
_____
_____

RESULTS
_____
_____

DISEASE
☐ YES   ☐ NO

TREATMENT USED
_____
_____

RESULTS
_____
_____

RATING
☆ ☆ ☆ ☆ ☆

SOWN FROM SEED

DATE SOWN	DAYS TO BLOOM/HARVEST
DATE GERMINATED	DATE BLOOMED /HARVESTED
DATE PLANTED OUT	TOTAL BLOOMS/HARVEST

TRANSPLANTED

DATE PLANTED	DATE BLOOMED/ HARVESTED
DATE OF FIRST BUD	TOTAL BLOOMS/HARVEST
DATE(S) OF PRUNING	DATE SPLIT/ TRANSPLANTED

IMPORTANT EVENTS/CHANGES
_____
_____
_____
_____
_____

NOTES
_____
_____
_____
_____
_____
_____

PLANT DESCRIPTION

[ ] #_____ NAME _____ SUPPLIER _____ PRICE _____
            #S

LIGHT REQUIREMENTS	WATERING REQUIREMENTS	ZONE HARDINESS	NEED TO OVERWINTER?
☀□ ☼□ ●□	◊ ◊◊ ◊◊◊ _____		[ ] YES [ ] NO DATE

NEW-TO-ME PLANT?   QTY   TYPE   [ ] FLOWER   [ ] FRUIT   [ ] VEGETABLE   [ ] HERB
                                      [ ] SHRUB   [ ] TREE   [ ] OTHER: _____
[ ] YES [ ] NO   _____ LIFE CYCLE [ ] ANNUAL [ ] BIENNIAL [ ] PERENNIAL

SOWN FROM SEED

DATE SOWN	DAYS TO BLOOM/HARVEST
DATE GERMINATED	DATE BLOOMED /HARVESTED
DATE PLANTED OUT	TOTAL BLOOMS/HARVEST

TRANSPLANTED

DATE PLANTED	DATE BLOOMED/ HARVESTED
DATE OF FIRST BUD	TOTAL BLOOMS/HARVEST
DATE(S) OF PRUNING	DATE SPLIT/ TRANSPLANTED

IMPORTANT EVENTS/CHANGES

_____
_____
_____
_____
_____

NOTES

_____
_____
_____
_____
_____
_____

GARDEN LOCATION(S)

_____

MATURE SIZE

_____   _____
HEIGHT   WIDTH

PRUNING REQUIRED?

[ ] YES   [ ] NO

PRUNING RATE

RARELY / SEASONALLY / REGULARLY

PESTS

[ ] YES   [ ] NO

TREATMENT USED

_____

RESULTS

_____

DISEASE

[ ] YES   [ ] NO

TREATMENT USED

_____

RESULTS

_____

RATING

☆☆☆☆☆   49

PLANT DESCRIPTION

☐ #_____ NAME _____ SUPPLIER #S _____ PRICE _____

LIGHT REQUIREMENTS	WATERING REQUIREMENTS	ZONE HARDINESS	NEED TO OVERWINTER?
☼ ☐ ☀ ☐ ☀ ☐	◊ ◊◊ ◊◊◊	_____	☐ YES ☐ NO DATE _____

NEW-TO-ME PLANT?   QTY

☐ YES ☐ NO   _____

TYPE
☐ FLOWER   ☐ FRUIT   ☐ VEGETABLE   ☐ HERB
☐ SHRUB   ☐ TREE   ☐ OTHER: _____

LIFE CYCLE   ☐ ANNUAL   ☐ BIENNIAL   ☐ PERENNIAL

GARDEN LOCATION(S)
_____
_____

MATURE SIZE

_____   _____
HEIGHT   WIDTH

PRUNING REQUIRED?

☐ YES   ☐ NO

PRUNING RATE

RARELY / SEASONALLY / REGULARLY

PESTS
☐ YES   ☐ NO

TREATMENT USED
_____
_____

RESULTS
_____
_____

DISEASE
☐ YES   ☐ NO

TREATMENT USED
_____
_____

RESULTS
_____
_____

RATING
☆☆☆☆☆

SOWN FROM SEED

DATE SOWN	DAYS TO BLOOM/HARVEST
DATE GERMINATED	DATE BLOOMED /HARVESTED
DATE PLANTED OUT	TOTAL BLOOMS/HARVEST

TRANSPLANTED

DATE PLANTED	DATE BLOOMED/ HARVESTED
DATE OF FIRST BUD	TOTAL BLOOMS/HARVEST
DATE(S) OF PRUNING	DATE SPLIT/ TRANSPLANTED

IMPORTANT EVENTS/CHANGES
_____
_____
_____
_____
_____
_____

NOTES
_____
_____
_____
_____
_____
_____

50

PLANT DESCRIPTION

_____ NAME _____ SUPPLIER #S _____ PRICE _____

LIGHT REQUIREMENTS ☼ ☐ ☀ ☐ ⬤ ☐   WATERING REQUIREMENTS ◌ ◌◌ ◌◌◌   ZONE HARDINESS _____   NEED TO OVERWINTER? ☐ YES ☐ NO   DATE _____

NEW-TO-ME PLANT? ☐ YES ☐ NO   QTY _____   TYPE   ☐ FLOWER ☐ SHRUB   ☐ FRUIT ☐ TREE   ☐ VEGETABLE ☐ OTHER: _____   ☐ HERB

LIFE CYCLE   ☐ ANNUAL   ☐ BIENNIAL   ☐ PERENNIAL

SOWN FROM SEED

DATE SOWN _____

DATE GERMINATED _____

DATE PLANTED OUT _____

DAYS TO BLOOM/HARVEST _____

DATE BLOOMED /HARVESTED _____

TOTAL BLOOMS/HARVEST _____

TRANSPLANTED

DATE PLANTED _____

DATE OF FIRST BUD _____

DATE(S) OF PRUNING _____

DATE BLOOMED/ HARVESTED _____

TOTAL BLOOMS/HARVEST _____

DATE SPLIT/ TRANSPLANTED _____

IMPORTANT EVENTS/CHANGES

_____

_____

_____

_____

_____

NOTES

_____

_____

_____

_____

_____

_____

GARDEN LOCATION(S)

_____

MATURE SIZE

_____   _____
HEIGHT   WIDTH

PRUNING REQUIRED?

☐ YES   ☐ NO

PRUNING RATE

RARELY / SEASONALLY / REGULARLY

PESTS

☐ YES   ☐ NO

TREATMENT USED

_____

RESULTS

_____

DISEASE

☐ YES   ☐ NO

TREATMENT USED

_____

RESULTS

_____

RATING

☆☆☆☆☆   51

PLANT DESCRIPTION

🌱 #_____ **NAME** _____ **SUPPLIER** #S _____ **PRICE** _____

LIGHT REQUIREMENTS ☼☐ 🌤☐ ☀☐   **WATERING REQUIREMENTS** 💧 💧💧 💧💧💧 _____   **ZONE HARDINESS**   **NEED TO OVERWINTER?** ☐ YES ☐ NO   DATE _____

NEW-TO-ME PLANT? ☐ YES ☐ NO   **QTY** _____   **TYPE** ☐ FLOWER ☐ SHRUB   ☐ FRUIT ☐ TREE   ☐ VEGETABLE ☐ OTHER: _____   ☐ HERB

LIFE CYCLE ☐ ANNUAL ☐ BIENNIAL ☐ PERENNIAL

GARDEN LOCATION(S)
_____
_____

MATURE SIZE
_____ _____
HEIGHT   WIDTH

PRUNING REQUIRED?
☐ YES   ☐ NO

PRUNING RATE
RARELY / SEASONALLY / REGULARLY

PESTS
☐ YES   ☐ NO

TREATMENT USED
_____
_____

RESULTS
_____
_____

DISEASE
☐ YES   ☐ NO

TREATMENT USED
_____
_____

RESULTS
_____
_____

RATING
☆☆☆☆☆

SOWN FROM SEED

DATE SOWN _____   DAYS TO BLOOM/HARVEST _____

DATE GERMINATED _____   DATE BLOOMED /HARVESTED _____

DATE PLANTED OUT _____   TOTAL BLOOMS/HARVEST _____

TRANSPLANTED

DATE PLANTED _____   DATE BLOOMED/ HARVESTED _____

DATE OF FIRST BUD _____   TOTAL BLOOMS/HARVEST _____

DATE(S) OF PRUNING _____   DATE SPLIT/ TRANSPLANTED _____

IMPORTANT EVENTS/CHANGES
_____
_____
_____
_____
_____
_____

NOTES
_____
_____
_____
_____
_____
_____

PLANT DESCRIPTION

🌱 #_____ NAME _____ SUPPLIER #S _____ PRICE _____

LIGHT REQUIREMENTS	WATERING REQUIREMENTS	ZONE HARDINESS	NEED TO OVERWINTER?
☼ ☐ 🌤 ☐ ☀ ☐	◊ ◊◊ ◊◊◊ _____		☐ YES ☐ NO DATE _____

NEW-TO-ME PLANT?   QTY   TYPE   ☐ FLOWER   ☐ FRUIT   ☐ VEGETABLE   ☐ HERB
                                   ☐ SHRUB   ☐ TREE   ☐ OTHER: _____

☐ YES ☐ NO   _____   LIFE CYCLE   ☐ ANNUAL   ☐ BIENNIAL   ☐ PERENNIAL

SOWN FROM SEED

DATE SOWN _____

DATE GERMINATED _____

DATE PLANTED OUT _____

DAYS TO BLOOM/HARVEST _____

DATE BLOOMED /HARVESTED _____

TOTAL BLOOMS/HARVEST _____

TRANSPLANTED

DATE PLANTED _____

DATE OF FIRST BUD _____

DATE(S) OF PRUNING _____

DATE BLOOMED/ HARVESTED _____

TOTAL BLOOMS/HARVEST _____

DATE SPLIT/ TRANSPLANTED _____

IMPORTANT EVENTS/CHANGES

_____
_____
_____
_____
_____

NOTES

_____
_____
_____
_____
_____

GARDEN LOCATION(S)

_____

MATURE SIZE

_____
HEIGHT   WIDTH

PRUNING REQUIRED?

☐ YES   ☐ NO

PRUNING RATE

RARELY / SEASONALLY / REGULARLY

PESTS

☐ YES   ☐ NO

TREATMENT USED

_____
_____

RESULTS

_____

DISEASE

☐ YES   ☐ NO

TREATMENT USED

_____
_____

RESULTS

_____

RATING

☆☆☆☆☆   53

PLANT DESCRIPTION

| # _____ | NAME _____ | SUPPLIER #S _____ | PRICE _____ |

LIGHT REQUIREMENTS	WATERING REQUIREMENTS	ZONE HARDINESS	NEED TO OVERWINTER?
☼ ☐ ☀ ☐ ☀ ☐	◌ ◌◌ ◌◌◌ _____		☐ YES ☐ NO DATE _____

NEW-TO-ME PLANT?
☐ YES ☐ NO

QTY _____

TYPE
☐ FLOWER ☐ FRUIT ☐ VEGETABLE ☐ HERB
☐ SHRUB ☐ TREE ☐ OTHER: _____

LIFE CYCLE
☐ ANNUAL ☐ BIENNIAL ☐ PERENNIAL

GARDEN LOCATION(S)
_____
_____

MATURE SIZE
_____   _____
HEIGHT   WIDTH

PRUNING REQUIRED?
☐ YES   ☐ NO

PRUNING RATE
RARELY / SEASONALLY / REGULARLY

PESTS
☐ YES   ☐ NO

TREATMENT USED
_____
_____

RESULTS
_____
_____

DISEASE
☐ YES   ☐ NO

TREATMENT USED
_____
_____

RESULTS
_____
_____

RATING
☆☆☆☆☆

SOWN FROM SEED

DATE SOWN _____	DAYS TO BLOOM/HARVEST _____
DATE GERMINATED _____	DATE BLOOMED /HARVESTED _____
DATE PLANTED OUT _____	TOTAL BLOOMS/HARVEST _____

TRANSPLANTED

DATE PLANTED _____	DATE BLOOMED/ HARVESTED _____
DATE OF FIRST BUD _____	TOTAL BLOOMS/HARVEST _____
DATE(S) OF PRUNING _____	DATE SPLIT/ TRANSPLANTED _____

IMPORTANT EVENTS/CHANGES
_____
_____
_____
_____
_____
_____

NOTES
_____
_____
_____
_____
_____
_____
_____

54

PLANT DESCRIPTION

____ NAME _____ SUPPLIER #S _____ PRICE _____

LIGHT REQUIREMENTS ☼ ☐ ☀ ☐ ☀ ☐

WATERING REQUIREMENTS ◊ ◊◊ ◊◊◊ _____

ZONE HARDINESS

NEED TO OVERWINTER?
☐ YES ☐ NO   DATE _____

NEW-TO-ME PLANT?
☐ YES ☐ NO

QTY _____

TYPE
☐ FLOWER ☐ FRUIT ☐ VEGETABLE ☐ HERB
☐ SHRUB ☐ TREE ☐ OTHER: _____

LIFE CYCLE ☐ ANNUAL ☐ BIENNIAL ☐ PERENNIAL

SOWN FROM SEED

DATE SOWN _____
DATE GERMINATED _____
DATE PLANTED OUT _____

DAYS TO BLOOM/HARVEST _____
DATE BLOOMED /HARVESTED _____
TOTAL BLOOMS/HARVEST _____

TRANSPLANTED

DATE PLANTED _____
DATE OF FIRST BUD _____
DATE(S) OF PRUNING _____

DATE BLOOMED/ HARVESTED _____
TOTAL BLOOMS/HARVEST _____
DATE SPLIT/ TRANSPLANTED _____

IMPORTANT EVENTS/CHANGES

_____
_____
_____
_____
_____
_____

NOTES

_____
_____
_____
_____
_____
_____

GARDEN LOCATION(S)

_____
_____

MATURE SIZE

_____ _____
HEIGHT   WIDTH

PRUNING REQUIRED?

☐ YES   ☐ NO

PRUNING RATE

RARELY / SEASONALLY / REGULARLY

PESTS

☐ YES   ☐ NO

TREATMENT USED
_____
_____

RESULTS
_____
_____

DISEASE

☐ YES   ☐ NO

TREATMENT USED
_____
_____

RESULTS
_____
_____

RATING

☆☆☆☆☆ 55

PLANT DESCRIPTION

_____ NAME _____ SUPPLIER #S _____ PRICE _____

LIGHT REQUIREMENTS	WATERING REQUIREMENTS	ZONE HARDINESS	NEED TO OVERWINTER?
☼ ☐ ☀ ☐ ☀ ☐	◌ ◌◌ ◌◌◌ _____		☐ YES ☐ NO DATE _____

NEW-TO-ME PLANT?   QTY   TYPE   ☐ FLOWER   ☐ FRUIT   ☐ VEGETABLE   ☐ HERB

☐ YES ☐ NO   _____   ☐ SHRUB   ☐ TREE   ☐ OTHER: _____

LIFE CYCLE   ☐ ANNUAL   ☐ BIENNIAL   ☐ PERENNIAL

GARDEN LOCATION(S)
_____

_____

MATURE SIZE

_____   _____
HEIGHT   WIDTH

PRUNING REQUIRED?

☐ YES   ☐ NO

PRUNING RATE

RARELY / SEASONALLY / REGULARLY

PESTS

☐ YES   ☐ NO

TREATMENT USED

_____

_____

RESULTS

_____

_____

DISEASE

☐ YES   ☐ NO

TREATMENT USED

_____

_____

RESULTS

_____

_____

RATING
☆☆☆☆☆

SOWN FROM SEED

DATE SOWN _____	DAYS TO BLOOM/HARVEST _____
DATE GERMINATED _____	DATE BLOOMED /HARVESTED _____
DATE PLANTED OUT _____	TOTAL BLOOMS/HARVEST _____

TRANSPLANTED

DATE PLANTED _____	DATE BLOOMED/ HARVESTED _____
DATE OF FIRST BUD _____	TOTAL BLOOMS/HARVEST _____
DATE(S) OF PRUNING _____	DATE SPLIT/ TRANSPLANTED _____

IMPORTANT EVENTS/CHANGES

_____

_____

_____

_____

_____

NOTES

_____

_____

_____

_____

_____

_____

PLANT DESCRIPTION

NAME   SUPPLIER   PRICE

\# _____   #S _____   _____

LIGHT REQUIREMENTS	WATERING REQUIREMENTS	ZONE HARDINESS	NEED TO OVERWINTER?
☼ ☐ ☀ ☐ ⬤ ☐	◊ ◊◊ ◊◊◊ _____		☐ YES ☐ NO DATE _____

NEW-TO-ME PLANT?   **QTY**   **TYPE**   ☐ FLOWER   ☐ FRUIT   ☐ VEGETABLE   ☐ HERB

☐ SHRUB   ☐ TREE   ☐ OTHER: _____

☐ YES ☐ NO   _____   **LIFE CYCLE**   ☐ ANNUAL   ☐ BIENNIAL   ☐ PERENNIAL

SOWN FROM SEED

DATE SOWN _____   DAYS TO BLOOM/HARVEST _____

DATE GERMINATED _____   DATE BLOOMED /HARVESTED _____

DATE PLANTED OUT _____   TOTAL BLOOMS/HARVEST _____

TRANSPLANTED

DATE PLANTED _____   DATE BLOOMED/ HARVESTED _____

DATE OF FIRST BUD _____   TOTAL BLOOMS/HARVEST _____

DATE(S) OF PRUNING _____   DATE SPLIT/ TRANSPLANTED _____

IMPORTANT EVENTS/CHANGES

_____
_____
_____
_____
_____

NOTES

_____
_____
_____
_____
_____
_____

GARDEN LOCATION(S)

_____
_____

MATURE SIZE

_____   _____
HEIGHT   WIDTH

PRUNING REQUIRED?

☐ YES   ☐ NO

PRUNING RATE

RARELY / SEASONALLY / REGULARLY

PESTS

☐ YES   ☐ NO

TREATMENT USED

_____
_____

RESULTS

_____
_____

DISEASE

☐ YES   ☐ NO

TREATMENT USED

_____
_____

RESULTS

_____
_____

RATING

☆☆☆☆☆   57

PLANT DESCRIPTION

☘ # _____ NAME _____ SUPPLIER #S _____ PRICE _____

LIGHT REQUIREMENTS ☼ ☐ 🌤 ☐ ☀ ☐

WATERING REQUIREMENTS ○ ○○ ○○○

ZONE HARDINESS _____

NEED TO OVERWINTER? ☐ YES ☐ NO DATE _____

NEW-TO-ME PLANT? ☐ YES ☐ NO

QTY _____

TYPE ☐ FLOWER ☐ SHRUB ☐ FRUIT ☐ TREE ☐ VEGETABLE ☐ OTHER: _____ ☐ HERB

LIFE CYCLE ☐ ANNUAL ☐ BIENNIAL ☐ PERENNIAL

GARDEN LOCATION(S)
_____
_____

MATURE SIZE
_____ _____
HEIGHT   WIDTH

PRUNING REQUIRED?
☐ YES ☐ NO

PRUNING RATE
RARELY / SEASONALLY / REGULARLY

PESTS
☐ YES ☐ NO

TREATMENT USED
_____
_____

RESULTS
_____
_____

DISEASE
☐ YES ☐ NO

TREATMENT USED
_____
_____

RESULTS
_____
_____

RATING
☆☆☆☆☆

SOWN FROM SEED

DATE SOWN _____ DAYS TO BLOOM/HARVEST _____

DATE GERMINATED _____ DATE BLOOMED /HARVESTED _____

DATE PLANTED OUT _____ TOTAL BLOOMS/HARVEST _____

TRANSPLANTED

DATE PLANTED _____ DATE BLOOMED/ HARVESTED _____

DATE OF FIRST BUD _____ TOTAL BLOOMS/HARVEST _____

DATE(S) OF PRUNING _____ DATE SPLIT/ TRANSPLANTED _____

IMPORTANT EVENTS/CHANGES
_____
_____
_____
_____
_____
_____

NOTES
_____
_____
_____
_____
_____

PLANT DESCRIPTION

___   NAME ___   SUPPLIER #S ___   PRICE ___

LIGHT REQUIREMENTS � ☐ ☀ ☐ ☀ ☐   WATERING REQUIREMENTS ◌ ◌◌ ◌◌◌   ZONE HARDINESS ___   NEED TO OVERWINTER? ☐ YES ☐ NO   DATE ___

NEW-TO-ME PLANT? ☐ YES ☐ NO   QTY ___   TYPE ☐ FLOWER ☐ SHRUB   ☐ FRUIT ☐ TREE   ☐ VEGETABLE ☐ OTHER: ___   ☐ HERB

LIFE CYCLE ☐ ANNUAL ☐ BIENNIAL ☐ PERENNIAL

SOWN FROM SEED

DATE SOWN ___   DAYS TO BLOOM/HARVEST ___

DATE GERMINATED ___   DATE BLOOMED /HARVESTED ___

DATE PLANTED OUT ___   TOTAL BLOOMS/HARVEST ___

TRANSPLANTED

DATE PLANTED ___   DATE BLOOMED/ HARVESTED ___

DATE OF FIRST BUD ___   TOTAL BLOOMS/HARVEST ___

DATE(S) OF PRUNING ___   DATE SPLIT/ TRANSPLANTED ___

IMPORTANT EVENTS/CHANGES

___
___
___
___
___

NOTES

___
___
___
___
___

GARDEN LOCATION(S)

___

MATURE SIZE

___
HEIGHT   WIDTH

PRUNING REQUIRED?
☐ YES   ☐ NO

PRUNING RATE
RARELY / SEASONALLY / REGULARLY

PESTS
☐ YES   ☐ NO

TREATMENT USED
___

RESULTS
___

DISEASE
☐ YES   ☐ NO

TREATMENT USED
___

RESULTS
___

RATING
☆☆☆☆☆   59

PLANT DESCRIPTION

_____   NAME _____   SUPPLIER _____   PRICE _____
#S

LIGHT REQUIREMENTS	WATERING REQUIREMENTS	ZONE HARDINESS	NEED TO OVERWINTER?
☼ ☐ ☀ ☐ ☀ ☐	◌ ◌◌ ◌◌◌	_____	☐ YES ☐ NO DATE _____

NEW-TO-ME PLANT?   QTY   TYPE   ☐ FLOWER   ☐ FRUIT   ☐ VEGETABLE   ☐ HERB
                                    ☐ SHRUB   ☐ TREE   ☐ OTHER: _____
☐ YES ☐ NO   _____   LIFE CYCLE   ☐ ANNUAL   ☐ BIENNIAL   ☐ PERENNIAL

GARDEN LOCATION(S)
_____
_____

MATURE SIZE
_____   _____
HEIGHT   WIDTH

PRUNING REQUIRED?
☐ YES   ☐ NO

PRUNING RATE
RARELY / SEASONALLY / REGULARLY

PESTS
☐ YES   ☐ NO

TREATMENT USED
_____
_____

RESULTS
_____
_____

DISEASE
☐ YES   ☐ NO

TREATMENT USED
_____
_____

RESULTS
_____
_____

RATING
☆☆☆☆☆

SOWN FROM SEED

DATE SOWN	DAYS TO BLOOM/HARVEST
DATE GERMINATED	DATE BLOOMED /HARVESTED
DATE PLANTED OUT	TOTAL BLOOMS/HARVEST

TRANSPLANTED

DATE PLANTED	DATE BLOOMED/ HARVESTED
DATE OF FIRST BUD	TOTAL BLOOMS/HARVEST
DATE(S) OF PRUNING	DATE SPLIT/ TRANSPLANTED

IMPORTANT EVENTS/CHANGES
_____
_____
_____
_____
_____
_____

NOTES
_____
_____
_____
_____
_____
_____

PLANT DESCRIPTION

🌱 # _____ NAME _____ SUPPLIER #S _____ PRICE _____

LIGHT REQUIREMENTS	WATERING REQUIREMENTS	ZONE HARDINESS	NEED TO OVERWINTER?
☼ ☐ 🌤 ☐ ☀ ☐	◊ ◊◊ ◊◊◊ _____		☐ YES ☐ NO DATE _____

NEW-TO-ME PLANT?   **QTY**   **TYPE**   ☐ FLOWER   ☐ FRUIT   ☐ VEGETABLE   ☐ HERB
☐ YES ☐ NO   _____   ☐ SHRUB   ☐ TREE   ☐ OTHER: _____

LIFE CYCLE   ☐ ANNUAL   ☐ BIENNIAL   ☐ PERENNIAL

SOWN FROM SEED

DATE SOWN _____

DATE GERMINATED _____

DATE PLANTED OUT _____

DAYS TO BLOOM/HARVEST _____

DATE BLOOMED /HARVESTED _____

TOTAL BLOOMS/HARVEST _____

TRANSPLANTED

DATE PLANTED _____

DATE OF FIRST BUD _____

DATE(S) OF PRUNING _____

DATE BLOOMED/ HARVESTED _____

TOTAL BLOOMS/HARVEST _____

DATE SPLIT/ TRANSPLANTED _____

IMPORTANT EVENTS/CHANGES

_____
_____
_____
_____
_____

NOTES

_____
_____
_____
_____
_____
_____

GARDEN LOCATION(S)

_____

_____

MATURE SIZE

_____   _____
HEIGHT   WIDTH

PRUNING REQUIRED?

☐ YES   ☐ NO

PRUNING RATE

RARELY / SEASONALLY / REGULARLY

PESTS

☐ YES   ☐ NO

TREATMENT USED

_____

_____

RESULTS

_____

_____

DISEASE

☐ YES   ☐ NO

TREATMENT USED

_____

_____

RESULTS

_____

_____

RATING

☆☆☆☆☆   61

PLANT DESCRIPTION

#_____   NAME _____   SUPPLIER #S _____   PRICE _____

LIGHT REQUIREMENTS	WATERING REQUIREMENTS	ZONE HARDINESS	NEED TO OVERWINTER?
☼ ☐ ☀ ☐ ☀ ☐	◊ ◊◊ ◊◊◊	_____	☐ YES ☐ NO DATE _____

NEW-TO-ME PLANT?   QTY

☐ YES ☐ NO   _____

TYPE ☐ FLOWER   ☐ FRUIT   ☐ VEGETABLE   ☐ HERB
      ☐ SHRUB   ☐ TREE   ☐ OTHER: _____

LIFE CYCLE ☐ ANNUAL   ☐ BIENNIAL   ☐ PERENNIAL

GARDEN LOCATION(S)
_____
_____

MATURE SIZE
_____
HEIGHT   WIDTH

PRUNING REQUIRED?
☐ YES   ☐ NO

PRUNING RATE
RARELY / SEASONALLY / REGULARLY

PESTS
☐ YES   ☐ NO

TREATMENT USED
_____
_____

RESULTS
_____
_____

DISEASE
☐ YES   ☐ NO

TREATMENT USED
_____
_____

RESULTS
_____
_____

RATING
☆☆☆☆☆

SOWN FROM SEED

DATE SOWN _____	DAYS TO BLOOM/HARVEST _____
DATE GERMINATED _____	DATE BLOOMED /HARVESTED _____
DATE PLANTED OUT _____	TOTAL BLOOMS/HARVEST _____

TRANSPLANTED

DATE PLANTED _____	DATE BLOOMED/ HARVESTED _____
DATE OF FIRST BUD _____	TOTAL BLOOMS/HARVEST _____
DATE(S) OF PRUNING _____	DATE SPLIT/ TRANSPLANTED _____

IMPORTANT EVENTS/CHANGES
_____
_____
_____
_____
_____

NOTES
_____
_____
_____
_____
_____
_____

PLANT DESCRIPTION

🌱 #_____   NAME _____   SUPPLIER #S _____   PRICE _____

LIGHT REQUIREMENTS	WATERING REQUIREMENTS	ZONE HARDINESS	NEED TO OVERWINTER?
☼ ☐ ✹ ☐ ⬤ ☐	◊ ◊◊ ◊◊◊	_____	☐ YES ☐ NO DATE _____

NEW-TO-ME PLANT?   QTY   TYPE   ☐ FLOWER   ☐ FRUIT   ☐ VEGETABLE   ☐ HERB

☐ YES ☐ NO   _____   ☐ SHRUB   ☐ TREE   ☐ OTHER: _____

LIFE CYCLE   ☐ ANNUAL   ☐ BIENNIAL   ☐ PERENNIAL

SOWN FROM SEED

DATE SOWN _____

DATE GERMINATED _____

DATE PLANTED OUT _____

DAYS TO BLOOM/HARVEST _____

DATE BLOOMED /HARVESTED _____

TOTAL BLOOMS/HARVEST _____

TRANSPLANTED

DATE PLANTED _____

DATE OF FIRST BUD _____

DATE(S) OF PRUNING _____

DATE BLOOMED/ HARVESTED _____

TOTAL BLOOMS/HARVEST _____

DATE SPLIT/ TRANSPLANTED _____

IMPORTANT EVENTS/CHANGES

_____

_____

_____

_____

_____

NOTES

_____

_____

_____

_____

_____

GARDEN LOCATION(S)
_____

MATURE SIZE

_____ _____
HEIGHT   WIDTH

PRUNING REQUIRED?

☐ YES   ☐ NO

PRUNING RATE

RARELY / SEASONALLY / REGULARLY

PESTS

☐ YES   ☐ NO

TREATMENT USED

_____

_____

RESULTS

_____

_____

DISEASE

☐ YES   ☐ NO

TREATMENT USED

_____

_____

RESULTS

_____

_____

RATING
☆☆☆☆☆ 63

PLANT DESCRIPTION

# _____	NAME _____

SUPPLIER
#S _____   PRICE _____

LIGHT REQUIREMENTS ☼ ☐ ☀ ☐ ☀ ☐   WATERING REQUIREMENTS ◌ ◌◌ ◌◌◌   ZONE HARDINESS _____   NEED TO OVERWINTER? ☐ YES ☐ NO   DATE _____

NEW-TO-ME PLANT?
☐ YES ☐ NO

QTY _____

TYPE
☐ FLOWER ☐ FRUIT ☐ VEGETABLE ☐ HERB
☐ SHRUB ☐ TREE ☐ OTHER: _____

LIFE CYCLE ☐ ANNUAL ☐ BIENNIAL ☐ PERENNIAL

GARDEN LOCATION(S)
_____
_____

MATURE SIZE
_____   _____
HEIGHT   WIDTH

PRUNING REQUIRED?
☐ YES   ☐ NO

PRUNING RATE
RARELY / SEASONALLY / REGULARLY

PESTS
☐ YES   ☐ NO

TREATMENT USED
_____
_____

RESULTS
_____
_____

DISEASE
☐ YES   ☐ NO

TREATMENT USED
_____
_____

RESULTS
_____
_____

RATING
☆☆☆☆☆

SOWN FROM SEED
DATE SOWN _____	DAYS TO BLOOM/HARVEST _____
DATE GERMINATED _____	DATE BLOOMED /HARVESTED _____
DATE PLANTED OUT _____	TOTAL BLOOMS/HARVEST _____

TRANSPLANTED
DATE PLANTED _____	DATE BLOOMED/ HARVESTED _____
DATE OF FIRST BUD _____	TOTAL BLOOMS/HARVEST _____
DATE(S) OF PRUNING _____	DATE SPLIT/ TRANSPLANTED _____

IMPORTANT EVENTS/CHANGES
_____
_____
_____
_____
_____
_____
_____

NOTES
_____
_____
_____
_____
_____
_____

PLANT DESCRIPTION

🌱 #_____   NAME _____   SUPPLIER #S _____   PRICE _____

LIGHT REQUIREMENTS ☼ ☐ ☀ ☐ ● ☐   **WATERING REQUIREMENTS** ◊ ◊◊ ◊◊◊ _____   **ZONE HARDINESS**   **NEED TO OVERWINTER?** ☐ YES ☐ NO   DATE _____

NEW-TO-ME PLANT? ☐ YES ☐ NO   **QTY** _____   **TYPE** ☐ FLOWER ☐ SHRUB   ☐ FRUIT ☐ TREE   ☐ VEGETABLE ☐ OTHER: _____   ☐ HERB

LIFE CYCLE ☐ ANNUAL ☐ BIENNIAL ☐ PERENNIAL

SOWN FROM SEED

DATE SOWN _____

DATE GERMINATED _____

DATE PLANTED OUT _____

DAYS TO BLOOM/HARVEST _____

DATE BLOOMED /HARVESTED _____

TOTAL BLOOMS/HARVEST _____

TRANSPLANTED

DATE PLANTED _____

DATE OF FIRST BUD _____

DATE(S) OF PRUNING _____

DATE BLOOMED/ HARVESTED _____

TOTAL BLOOMS/HARVEST _____

DATE SPLIT/ TRANSPLANTED _____

IMPORTANT EVENTS/CHANGES

_____

_____

_____

_____

NOTES

_____

_____

_____

_____

_____

GARDEN LOCATION(S)

_____

_____

MATURE SIZE

_____

HEIGHT   WIDTH

PRUNING REQUIRED?

☐ YES   ☐ NO

PRUNING RATE

RARELY / SEASONALLY / REGULARLY

PESTS

☐ YES   ☐ NO

TREATMENT USED

_____

_____

RESULTS

_____

_____

DISEASE

☐ YES   ☐ NO

TREATMENT USED

_____

_____

RESULTS

_____

_____

RATING

☆ ☆ ☆ ☆ ☆   65

PLANT DESCRIPTION

_____ NAME _____ SUPPLIER #S _____ PRICE _____

LIGHT REQUIREMENTS ☼ ☐ ☀ ☐ ☀ ☐   WATERING REQUIREMENTS 💧 💧💧 💧💧💧 _____   ZONE HARDINESS   NEED TO OVERWINTER? ☐ YES ☐ NO   DATE _____

NEW-TO-ME PLANT? ☐ YES ☐ NO   QTY _____   TYPE ☐ FLOWER ☐ SHRUB   ☐ FRUIT ☐ TREE   ☐ VEGETABLE ☐ OTHER: _____   ☐ HERB

LIFE CYCLE ☐ ANNUAL ☐ BIENNIAL ☐ PERENNIAL

GARDEN LOCATION(S)
_____
_____

MATURE SIZE
_____ _____
HEIGHT   WIDTH

PRUNING REQUIRED?
☐ YES   ☐ NO

PRUNING RATE
RARELY / SEASONALLY / REGULARLY

PESTS
☐ YES   ☐ NO

TREATMENT USED
_____
_____

RESULTS
_____
_____

DISEASE
☐ YES   ☐ NO

TREATMENT USED
_____
_____

RESULTS
_____
_____

RATING
☆☆☆☆☆

SOWN FROM SEED

DATE SOWN	DAYS TO BLOOM/HARVEST
DATE GERMINATED	DATE BLOOMED /HARVESTED
DATE PLANTED OUT	TOTAL BLOOMS/HARVEST

TRANSPLANTED

DATE PLANTED	DATE BLOOMED/ HARVESTED
DATE OF FIRST BUD	TOTAL BLOOMS/HARVEST
DATE(S) OF PRUNING	DATE SPLIT/ TRANSPLANTED

IMPORTANT EVENTS/CHANGES
_____
_____
_____
_____
_____

NOTES
_____
_____
_____
_____
_____
_____

PLANT DESCRIPTION

_____ **NAME** _____ **SUPPLIER #S** _____ **PRICE** _____

LIGHT REQUIREMENTS	WATERING REQUIREMENTS	ZONE HARDINESS	NEED TO OVERWINTER?
☼ ☐ ☀ ☐ ☀ ☐	⬭ ⬭⬭ ⬭⬭⬭ _____		☐ YES ☐ NO DATE _____

NEW-TO-ME PLANT? ☐ YES ☐ NO

QTY _____

TYPE ☐ FLOWER ☐ FRUIT ☐ VEGETABLE ☐ HERB ☐ SHRUB ☐ TREE ☐ OTHER: _____

LIFE CYCLE ☐ ANNUAL ☐ BIENNIAL ☐ PERENNIAL

SOWN FROM SEED

DATE SOWN

DATE GERMINATED

DATE PLANTED OUT

DAYS TO BLOOM/HARVEST

DATE BLOOMED /HARVESTED

TOTAL BLOOMS/HARVEST

TRANSPLANTED

DATE PLANTED

DATE OF FIRST BUD

DATE(S) OF PRUNING

DATE BLOOMED/ HARVESTED

TOTAL BLOOMS/HARVEST

DATE SPLIT/ TRANSPLANTED

IMPORTANT EVENTS/CHANGES

NOTES

GARDEN LOCATION(S)

MATURE SIZE

HEIGHT   WIDTH

PRUNING REQUIRED?

☐ YES   ☐ NO

PRUNING RATE

RARELY / SEASONALLY / REGULARLY

PESTS

☐ YES   ☐ NO

TREATMENT USED

RESULTS

DISEASE

☐ YES   ☐ NO

TREATMENT USED

RESULTS

RATING

☆☆☆☆☆ 67

PLANT DESCRIPTION

_____ **NAME** _____ **SUPPLIER #S** _____ **PRICE** _____

LIGHT REQUIREMENTS ☼ ☐ ☀ ☐ ☀ ☐

WATERING REQUIREMENTS ⬤ ⬤⬤ ⬤⬤⬤

ZONE HARDINESS _____

NEED TO OVERWINTER? ☐ YES ☐ NO DATE

NEW-TO-ME PLANT?
☐ YES ☐ NO

QTY _____

TYPE
☐ FLOWER ☐ FRUIT ☐ VEGETABLE ☐ HERB
☐ SHRUB ☐ TREE ☐ OTHER: _____

LIFE CYCLE ☐ ANNUAL ☐ BIENNIAL ☐ PERENNIAL

GARDEN LOCATION(S)
_____
_____

MATURE SIZE
_____ _____
HEIGHT WIDTH

PRUNING REQUIRED?
☐ YES ☐ NO

PRUNING RATE
RARELY / SEASONALLY / REGULARLY

PESTS
☐ YES ☐ NO

TREATMENT USED
_____
_____

RESULTS
_____
_____

DISEASE
☐ YES ☐ NO

TREATMENT USED
_____
_____

RESULTS
_____
_____

RATING
☆☆☆☆☆

SOWN FROM SEED

DATE SOWN	DAYS TO BLOOM/HARVEST
DATE GERMINATED	DATE BLOOMED /HARVESTED
DATE PLANTED OUT	TOTAL BLOOMS/HARVEST

TRANSPLANTED

DATE PLANTED	DATE BLOOMED/ HARVESTED
DATE OF FIRST BUD	TOTAL BLOOMS/HARVEST
DATE(S) OF PRUNING	DATE SPLIT/ TRANSPLANTED

IMPORTANT EVENTS/CHANGES
_____
_____
_____
_____
_____
_____

NOTES
_____
_____
_____
_____
_____
_____

PLANT DESCRIPTION

#_____ NAME _____ SUPPLIER #S _____ PRICE _____

LIGHT REQUIREMENTS ☼ ☐ ☀ ☐ ● ☐   WATERING REQUIREMENTS ◊ ◊◊ ◊◊◊   ZONE HARDINESS _____   NEED TO OVERWINTER? ☐ YES ☐ NO   DATE _____

NEW-TO-ME PLANT? QTY TYPE ☐ FLOWER ☐ FRUIT ☐ VEGETABLE ☐ HERB
                                      ☐ SHRUB ☐ TREE ☐ OTHER: _____
☐ YES ☐ NO _____ LIFE CYCLE ☐ ANNUAL ☐ BIENNIAL ☐ PERENNIAL

SOWN FROM SEED

DATE SOWN

DATE GERMINATED

DATE PLANTED OUT

DAYS TO BLOOM/HARVEST

DATE BLOOMED /HARVESTED

TOTAL BLOOMS/HARVEST

TRANSPLANTED

DATE PLANTED

DATE OF FIRST BUD

DATE(S) OF PRUNING

DATE BLOOMED/ HARVESTED

TOTAL BLOOMS/HARVEST

DATE SPLIT/ TRANSPLANTED

IMPORTANT EVENTS/CHANGES

_____
_____
_____
_____
_____

NOTES

_____
_____
_____
_____
_____

GARDEN LOCATION(S)

_____

MATURE SIZE

_____ _____
HEIGHT   WIDTH

PRUNING REQUIRED?
☐ YES   ☐ NO

PRUNING RATE
RARELY / SEASONALLY / REGULARLY

PESTS
☐ YES   ☐ NO

TREATMENT USED
_____

RESULTS
_____

DISEASE
☐ YES   ☐ NO

TREATMENT USED
_____

RESULTS
_____

RATING
☆☆☆☆☆ 69

PLANT DESCRIPTION

NAME   SUPPLIER   PRICE

\# _____ #S _____ _____

LIGHT   WATERING   ZONE   NEED TO OVERWINTER?
REQUIREMENTS REQUIREMENTS   HARDINESS
☼ ☐ ☀ ☐ ● ☐   ◊ ◊◊ ◊◊◊ _____   ☐ YES ☐ NO   DATE _____

NEW-TO-ME   QTY   TYPE   ☐ FLOWER   ☐ FRUIT   ☐ VEGETABLE   ☐ HERB
PLANT?   ☐ SHRUB   ☐ TREE   ☐ OTHER: _____
☐ YES ☐ NO   _____   LIFE CYCLE ☐ ANNUAL ☐ BIENNIAL ☐ PERENNIAL

GARDEN LOCATION(S)
_____

_____

MATURE SIZE
_____   _____
HEIGHT   WIDTH

PRUNING REQUIRED?
☐ YES   ☐ NO

PRUNING RATE
RARELY / SEASONALLY / REGULARLY

PESTS
☐ YES   ☐ NO

TREATMENT USED

_____

_____

RESULTS

_____

_____

DISEASE
☐ YES   ☐ NO

TREATMENT USED

_____

_____

RESULTS

_____

_____

RATING
☆☆☆☆☆

70

SOWN FROM SEED

DATE SOWN _____

DATE GERMINATED _____

DATE PLANTED OUT _____

DAYS TO BLOOM/HARVEST _____

DATE BLOOMED /HARVESTED _____

TOTAL BLOOMS/HARVEST _____

TRANSPLANTED

DATE PLANTED _____

DATE OF FIRST BUD _____

DATE(S) OF PRUNING _____

DATE BLOOMED/ HARVESTED _____

TOTAL BLOOMS/HARVEST _____

DATE SPLIT/ TRANSPLANTED _____

IMPORTANT EVENTS/CHANGES

_____

_____

_____

_____

_____

_____

NOTES

_____

_____

_____

_____

_____

_____

PLANT DESCRIPTION

___   NAME ___   SUPPLIER #S ___   PRICE ___

LIGHT REQUIREMENTS   ☼ ☐ ☀ ☐ ☀ ☐

WATERING REQUIREMENTS   ◌ ◌◌ ◌◌◌

ZONE HARDINESS ___

NEED TO OVERWINTER?   ☐ YES ☐ NO   DATE ___

NEW-TO-ME PLANT?   ☐ YES ☐ NO

QTY ___

TYPE
☐ FLOWER   ☐ FRUIT   ☐ VEGETABLE   ☐ HERB
☐ SHRUB   ☐ TREE   ☐ OTHER: ___

LIFE CYCLE   ☐ ANNUAL   ☐ BIENNIAL   ☐ PERENNIAL

SOWN FROM SEED

DATE SOWN ___

DAYS TO BLOOM/HARVEST ___

DATE GERMINATED ___

DATE BLOOMED /HARVESTED ___

DATE PLANTED OUT ___

TOTAL BLOOMS/HARVEST ___

TRANSPLANTED

DATE PLANTED ___

DATE BLOOMED/ HARVESTED ___

DATE OF FIRST BUD ___

TOTAL BLOOMS/HARVEST ___

DATE(S) OF PRUNING ___

DATE SPLIT/ TRANSPLANTED ___

IMPORTANT EVENTS/CHANGES

___
___
___
___
___

NOTES

___
___
___
___
___
___

GARDEN LOCATION(S)

___

MATURE SIZE

___ ___
HEIGHT   WIDTH

PRUNING REQUIRED?

☐ YES   ☐ NO

PRUNING RATE

RARELY / SEASONALLY / REGULARLY

PESTS

☐ YES   ☐ NO

TREATMENT USED

___
___

RESULTS

___

DISEASE

☐ YES   ☐ NO

TREATMENT USED

___
___

RESULTS

___
___

RATING

☆☆☆☆☆   71

PLANT DESCRIPTION

🌱 #_____   NAME _____   SUPPLIER #S _____   PRICE _____

LIGHT REQUIREMENTS	WATERING REQUIREMENTS	ZONE HARDINESS	NEED TO OVERWINTER?
☀️☐ 🌤️☐ 🌞☐	💧 💧💧 💧💧💧 _____		☐ YES ☐ NO DATE _____

NEW-TO-ME PLANT?   QTY   TYPE   ☐ FLOWER   ☐ FRUIT   ☐ VEGETABLE   ☐ HERB
☐ YES ☐ NO   _____   ☐ SHRUB   ☐ TREE   ☐ OTHER: _____
                              LIFE CYCLE   ☐ ANNUAL   ☐ BIENNIAL   ☐ PERENNIAL

GARDEN LOCATION(S)
_____
_____

MATURE SIZE
_____   _____
HEIGHT   WIDTH

PRUNING REQUIRED?
☐ YES   ☐ NO

PRUNING RATE
RARELY / SEASONALLY / REGULARLY

PESTS
☐ YES   ☐ NO

TREATMENT USED
_____
_____

RESULTS
_____
_____

DISEASE
☐ YES   ☐ NO

TREATMENT USED
_____
_____

RESULTS
_____
_____

SOWN FROM SEED

DATE SOWN _____	DAYS TO BLOOM/HARVEST _____
DATE GERMINATED _____	DATE BLOOMED /HARVESTED _____
DATE PLANTED OUT _____	TOTAL BLOOMS/HARVEST _____

TRANSPLANTED

DATE PLANTED _____	DATE BLOOMED/ HARVESTED _____
DATE OF FIRST BUD _____	TOTAL BLOOMS/HARVEST _____
DATE(S) OF PRUNING _____	DATE SPLIT/ TRANSPLANTED _____

IMPORTANT EVENTS/CHANGES
_____
_____
_____
_____
_____
_____

NOTES
_____
_____
_____
_____
_____
_____

RATING
☆☆☆☆☆

PLANT DESCRIPTION

NAME   SUPPLIER   PRICE
#S

LIGHT REQUIREMENTS ☼ ☐ ☀ ☐ ☀ ☐   WATERING REQUIREMENTS ◊ ◊◊ ◊◊◊   ZONE HARDINESS   NEED TO OVERWINTER? ☐ YES ☐ NO   DATE

NEW-TO-ME PLANT?   QTY   TYPE   ☐ FLOWER   ☐ FRUIT   ☐ VEGETABLE   ☐ HERB
                                   ☐ SHRUB   ☐ TREE   ☐ OTHER: _____
☐ YES ☐ NO   _____   LIFE CYCLE   ☐ ANNUAL   ☐ BIENNIAL   ☐ PERENNIAL

SOWN FROM SEED

DATE SOWN

DATE GERMINATED

DATE PLANTED OUT

DAYS TO BLOOM/HARVEST

DATE BLOOMED /HARVESTED

TOTAL BLOOMS/HARVEST

TRANSPLANTED

DATE PLANTED

DATE OF FIRST BUD

DATE(S) OF PRUNING

DATE BLOOMED/ HARVESTED

TOTAL BLOOMS/HARVEST

DATE SPLIT/ TRANSPLANTED

IMPORTANT EVENTS/CHANGES

NOTES

GARDEN LOCATION(S)

MATURE SIZE

HEIGHT   WIDTH

PRUNING REQUIRED?
☐ YES   ☐ NO

PRUNING RATE
RARELY / SEASONALLY / REGULARLY

PESTS
☐ YES   ☐ NO

TREATMENT USED

RESULTS

DISEASE
☐ YES   ☐ NO

TREATMENT USED

RESULTS

RATING
☆☆☆☆☆   73

PLANT DESCRIPTION

NAME | SUPPLIER | PRICE
#_____ | #S |

LIGHT REQUIREMENTS ☼ ☐ ☀ ☐ ☀ ☐   **WATERING REQUIREMENTS** ◊ ◊◊ ◊◊◊   **ZONE HARDINESS** _____   **NEED TO OVERWINTER?** ☐ YES ☐ NO   DATE

NEW-TO-ME PLANT? ☐ YES ☐ NO

QTY _____

TYPE ☐ FLOWER ☐ SHRUB ☐ FRUIT ☐ TREE ☐ VEGETABLE ☐ OTHER: _____ ☐ HERB

LIFE CYCLE ☐ ANNUAL ☐ BIENNIAL ☐ PERENNIAL

GARDEN LOCATION(S)
_____
_____

MATURE SIZE
_____ _____
HEIGHT   WIDTH

PRUNING REQUIRED?
☐ YES   ☐ NO

PRUNING RATE
RARELY / SEASONALLY / REGULARLY

PESTS
☐ YES   ☐ NO

TREATMENT USED
_____
_____

RESULTS
_____
_____

DISEASE
☐ YES   ☐ NO

TREATMENT USED
_____
_____

RESULTS
_____
_____

RATING
☆☆☆☆☆

SOWN FROM SEED
DATE SOWN _____ | DAYS TO BLOOM/HARVEST _____
DATE GERMINATED _____ | DATE BLOOMED /HARVESTED _____
DATE PLANTED OUT _____ | TOTAL BLOOMS/HARVEST _____

TRANSPLANTED
DATE PLANTED _____ | DATE BLOOMED/ HARVESTED _____
DATE OF FIRST BUD _____ | TOTAL BLOOMS/HARVEST _____
DATE(S) OF PRUNING _____ | DATE SPLIT/ TRANSPLANTED _____

IMPORTANT EVENTS/CHANGES
_____
_____
_____
_____
_____
_____

NOTES
_____
_____
_____
_____
_____
_____
_____

74

PLANT DESCRIPTION

🌱 # NAME _____ SUPPLIER #S _____ PRICE _____

LIGHT REQUIREMENTS	WATERING REQUIREMENTS	ZONE HARDINESS	NEED TO OVERWINTER?
☼ ☐ ☀ ☐ ☀ ☐	◌ ◌◌ ◌◌◌ _____		☐ YES ☐ NO DATE _____

NEW-TO-ME PLANT?   QTY   TYPE   ☐ FLOWER   ☐ FRUIT   ☐ VEGETABLE   ☐ HERB
                                 ☐ SHRUB   ☐ TREE   ☐ OTHER: _____

☐ YES ☐ NO   _____   LIFE CYCLE   ☐ ANNUAL   ☐ BIENNIAL   ☐ PERENNIAL

SOWN FROM SEED

DATE SOWN _____

DAYS TO BLOOM/HARVEST _____

DATE GERMINATED _____

DATE BLOOMED /HARVESTED _____

DATE PLANTED OUT _____

TOTAL BLOOMS/HARVEST _____

TRANSPLANTED

DATE PLANTED _____

DATE BLOOMED/ HARVESTED _____

DATE OF FIRST BUD _____

TOTAL BLOOMS/HARVEST _____

DATE(S) OF PRUNING _____

DATE SPLIT/ TRANSPLANTED _____

IMPORTANT EVENTS/CHANGES

_____
_____
_____
_____
_____
_____

NOTES

_____
_____
_____
_____
_____

GARDEN LOCATION(S)

_____

MATURE SIZE

_____
HEIGHT   WIDTH

PRUNING REQUIRED?

☐ YES   ☐ NO

PRUNING RATE

RARELY / SEASONALLY / REGULARLY

PESTS

☐ YES   ☐ NO

TREATMENT USED

_____

RESULTS

_____

DISEASE

☐ YES   ☐ NO

TREATMENT USED

_____

RESULTS

_____

RATING

☆☆☆☆☆   75

PLANT DESCRIPTION

__ NAME _____ SUPPLIER _____ PRICE _____
                            #S

LIGHT REQUIREMENTS	WATERING REQUIREMENTS	ZONE HARDINESS	NEED TO OVERWINTER?
☼ ☐ ❉ ☐ ☀ ☐	◊ ◊◊ ◊◊◊ _____		☐ YES ☐ NO DATE _____

NEW-TO-ME PLANT? **QTY** **TYPE** ☐ FLOWER ☐ FRUIT ☐ VEGETABLE ☐ HERB

☐ YES ☐ NO _____ ☐ SHRUB ☐ TREE ☐ OTHER: _____

LIFE CYCLE ☐ ANNUAL ☐ BIENNIAL ☐ PERENNIAL

GARDEN LOCATION(S)
_____
_____

MATURE SIZE
_____ _____
HEIGHT   WIDTH

PRUNING REQUIRED?
☐ YES   ☐ NO

PRUNING RATE
RARELY / SEASONALLY / REGULARLY

PESTS
☐ YES   ☐ NO

TREATMENT USED
_____
_____

RESULTS
_____
_____

DISEASE
☐ YES   ☐ NO

TREATMENT USED
_____
_____

RESULTS
_____
_____

SOWN FROM SEED

DATE SOWN	DAYS TO BLOOM/HARVEST
DATE GERMINATED	DATE BLOOMED /HARVESTED
DATE PLANTED OUT	TOTAL BLOOMS/HARVEST

TRANSPLANTED

DATE PLANTED	DATE BLOOMED/ HARVESTED
DATE OF FIRST BUD	TOTAL BLOOMS/HARVEST
DATE(S) OF PRUNING	DATE SPLIT/ TRANSPLANTED

IMPORTANT EVENTS/CHANGES
_____
_____
_____
_____
_____

NOTES
_____
_____
_____
_____
_____
_____

RATING
☆☆☆☆☆

PLANT DESCRIPTION

_____ NAME _____ SUPPLIER #S _____ PRICE _____

LIGHT REQUIREMENTS ☼ ☐ ☀ ☐ ● ☐   WATERING REQUIREMENTS ◌ ◌◌ ◌◌◌   ZONE HARDINESS _____   NEED TO OVERWINTER? ☐ YES ☐ NO   DATE _____

NEW-TO-ME PLANT?   QTY   TYPE   ☐ FLOWER   ☐ FRUIT   ☐ VEGETABLE   ☐ HERB
                                ☐ SHRUB   ☐ TREE   ☐ OTHER: _____
☐ YES ☐ NO   _____   LIFE CYCLE   ☐ ANNUAL   ☐ BIENNIAL   ☐ PERENNIAL

SOWN FROM SEED

DATE SOWN _____

DATE GERMINATED _____

DATE PLANTED OUT _____

DAYS TO BLOOM/HARVEST _____

DATE BLOOMED /HARVESTED _____

TOTAL BLOOMS/HARVEST _____

TRANSPLANTED

DATE PLANTED _____

DATE OF FIRST BUD _____

DATE(S) OF PRUNING _____

DATE BLOOMED/ HARVESTED _____

TOTAL BLOOMS/HARVEST _____

DATE SPLIT/ TRANSPLANTED _____

IMPORTANT EVENTS/CHANGES

_____

_____

_____

_____

_____

NOTES

_____

_____

_____

_____

_____

_____

GARDEN LOCATION(S)

_____

MATURE SIZE

_____
HEIGHT   WIDTH

PRUNING REQUIRED?

☐ YES   ☐ NO

PRUNING RATE

RARELY / SEASONALLY / REGULARLY

PESTS

☐ YES   ☐ NO

TREATMENT USED

_____

RESULTS

_____

DISEASE

☐ YES   ☐ NO

TREATMENT USED

_____

RESULTS

_____

RATING
☆☆☆☆☆ 77

PLANT DESCRIPTION

🌱 #_____ NAME _____ SUPPLIER #S _____ PRICE _____

LIGHT REQUIREMENTS	WATERING REQUIREMENTS	ZONE HARDINESS	NEED TO OVERWINTER?
☼ ☐ ☀ ☐ ⬤ ☐	💧 💧💧 💧💧💧	_____	☐ YES ☐ NO DATE

NEW-TO-ME PLANT? QTY TYPE ☐ FLOWER ☐ FRUIT ☐ VEGETABLE ☐ HERB
☐ YES ☐ NO _____ ☐ SHRUB ☐ TREE ☐ OTHER: _____
LIFE CYCLE ☐ ANNUAL ☐ BIENNIAL ☐ PERENNIAL

GARDEN LOCATION(S)
_____

_____

MATURE SIZE

_____ _____
HEIGHT WIDTH

PRUNING REQUIRED?
☐ YES ☐ NO

PRUNING RATE
RARELY / SEASONALLY / REGULARLY

PESTS
☐ YES ☐ NO

TREATMENT USED
_____

_____

RESULTS
_____

_____

DISEASE
☐ YES ☐ NO

TREATMENT USED
_____

_____

RESULTS
_____

_____

RATING
☆☆☆☆☆

SOWN FROM SEED

DATE SOWN	DAYS TO BLOOM/HARVEST
DATE GERMINATED	DATE BLOOMED /HARVESTED
DATE PLANTED OUT	TOTAL BLOOMS/HARVEST

TRANSPLANTED

DATE PLANTED	DATE BLOOMED/ HARVESTED
DATE OF FIRST BUD	TOTAL BLOOMS/HARVEST
DATE(S) OF PRUNING	DATE SPLIT/ TRANSPLANTED

IMPORTANT EVENTS/CHANGES
_____

_____

_____

_____

_____

_____

NOTES
_____

_____

_____

_____

_____

_____

PLANT DESCRIPTION

____   NAME _____   SUPPLIER #S _____   PRICE _____

LIGHT REQUIREMENTS ☼ ☐ ☀ ☐ ☀ ☐

WATERING REQUIREMENTS ◌ ◌◌ ◌◌◌ _____

ZONE HARDINESS _____

NEED TO OVERWINTER? ☐ YES ☐ NO   DATE

NEW-TO-ME PLANT? ☐ YES ☐ NO

QTY _____

TYPE
☐ FLOWER ☐ FRUIT ☐ VEGETABLE ☐ HERB
☐ SHRUB ☐ TREE ☐ OTHER:

LIFE CYCLE ☐ ANNUAL ☐ BIENNIAL ☐ PERENNIAL

SOWN FROM SEED

DATE SOWN _____

DATE GERMINATED _____

DATE PLANTED OUT _____

DAYS TO BLOOM/HARVEST _____

DATE BLOOMED /HARVESTED _____

TOTAL BLOOMS/HARVEST _____

TRANSPLANTED

DATE PLANTED _____

DATE OF FIRST BUD _____

DATE(S) OF PRUNING _____

DATE BLOOMED/ HARVESTED _____

TOTAL BLOOMS/HARVEST _____

DATE SPLIT/ TRANSPLANTED _____

IMPORTANT EVENTS/CHANGES

_____

_____

_____

_____

_____

NOTES

_____

_____

_____

_____

_____

_____

GARDEN LOCATION(S)

_____

_____

MATURE SIZE

_____   _____
HEIGHT   WIDTH

PRUNING REQUIRED?

☐ YES   ☐ NO

PRUNING RATE

RARELY / SEASONALLY / REGULARLY

PESTS

☐ YES   ☐ NO

TREATMENT USED

_____

RESULTS

_____

DISEASE

☐ YES   ☐ NO

TREATMENT USED

_____

RESULTS

_____

RATING

☆☆☆☆☆   79

PLANT DESCRIPTION

___ NAME _____ SUPPLIER #S _____ PRICE _____

LIGHT REQUIREMENTS	WATERING REQUIREMENTS	ZONE HARDINESS	NEED TO OVERWINTER?
☼ ☐ ☀ ☐ ☀ ☐	◌ ◌◌ ◌◌◌ _____		☐ YES ☐ NO DATE _____

NEW-TO-ME PLANT?   **QTY**

☐ YES ☐ NO   _____

TYPE
☐ FLOWER   ☐ FRUIT   ☐ VEGETABLE   ☐ HERB
☐ SHRUB   ☐ TREE   ☐ OTHER: _____

LIFE CYCLE ☐ ANNUAL   ☐ BIENNIAL   ☐ PERENNIAL

GARDEN LOCATION(S)
_____
_____

MATURE SIZE
_____
HEIGHT   WIDTH

PRUNING REQUIRED?
☐ YES   ☐ NO

PRUNING RATE
RARELY / SEASONALLY / REGULARLY

PESTS
☐ YES   ☐ NO

TREATMENT USED
_____
_____

RESULTS
_____
_____

DISEASE
☐ YES   ☐ NO

TREATMENT USED
_____
_____

RESULTS
_____
_____

RATING
☆☆☆☆☆

SOWN FROM SEED
DATE SOWN _____	DAYS TO BLOOM/HARVEST _____
DATE GERMINATED _____	DATE BLOOMED /HARVESTED _____
DATE PLANTED OUT _____	TOTAL BLOOMS/HARVEST _____

TRANSPLANTED
DATE PLANTED _____	DATE BLOOMED/ HARVESTED _____
DATE OF FIRST BUD _____	TOTAL BLOOMS/HARVEST _____
DATE(S) OF PRUNING _____	DATE SPLIT/ TRANSPLANTED _____

IMPORTANT EVENTS/CHANGES
_____
_____
_____
_____
_____
_____

NOTES
_____
_____
_____
_____
_____

PLANT DESCRIPTION

🌱 #_____ NAME _____ SUPPLIER #S _____ PRICE _____

LIGHT REQUIREMENTS	WATERING REQUIREMENTS	ZONE HARDINESS	NEED TO OVERWINTER?
☼ ☐ ☀ ☐ ● ☐	◊ ◊◊ ◊◊◊	_____	☐ YES ☐ NO DATE _____

NEW-TO-ME PLANT? **QTY** **TYPE**   ☐ FLOWER ☐ FRUIT ☐ VEGETABLE ☐ HERB

☐ YES ☐ NO   _____   ☐ SHRUB   ☐ TREE   ☐ OTHER: _____

LIFE CYCLE   ☐ ANNUAL ☐ BIENNIAL ☐ PERENNIAL

SOWN FROM SEED

DATE SOWN _____

DATE GERMINATED _____

DATE PLANTED OUT _____

DAYS TO BLOOM/HARVEST _____

DATE BLOOMED /HARVESTED _____

TOTAL BLOOMS/HARVEST _____

TRANSPLANTED

DATE PLANTED _____

DATE OF FIRST BUD _____

DATE(S) OF PRUNING _____

DATE BLOOMED/ HARVESTED _____

TOTAL BLOOMS/HARVEST _____

DATE SPLIT/ TRANSPLANTED _____

IMPORTANT EVENTS/CHANGES

_____

_____

_____

_____

_____

NOTES

_____

_____

_____

_____

_____

GARDEN LOCATION(S)

_____

_____

MATURE SIZE

_____ _____
HEIGHT   WIDTH

PRUNING REQUIRED?

☐ YES   ☐ NO

PRUNING RATE

RARELY / SEASONALLY / REGULARLY

PESTS

☐ YES   ☐ NO

TREATMENT USED

_____

_____

RESULTS

_____

_____

DISEASE

☐ YES   ☐ NO

TREATMENT USED

_____

_____

RESULTS

_____

RATING

☆☆☆☆☆   81

PLANT DESCRIPTION

[🌱] #_____   NAME _____   SUPPLIER #S _____   PRICE _____

LIGHT REQUIREMENTS	WATERING REQUIREMENTS	ZONE HARDINESS	NEED TO OVERWINTER?
☼ ☐ ☀ ☐ ● ☐	◌ ◌◌ ◌◌◌	_____	☐ YES ☐ NO DATE

NEW-TO-ME PLANT?   **QTY**

☐ YES ☐ NO   _____

TYPE
☐ FLOWER ☐ FRUIT ☐ VEGETABLE ☐ HERB
☐ SHRUB   ☐ TREE   ☐ OTHER: _____

LIFE CYCLE ☐ ANNUAL ☐ BIENNIAL ☐ PERENNIAL

GARDEN LOCATION(S)
_____
_____

MATURE SIZE
_____ _____
HEIGHT   WIDTH

PRUNING REQUIRED?
☐ YES   ☐ NO

PRUNING RATE
RARELY / SEASONALLY / REGULARLY

PESTS
☐ YES   ☐ NO

TREATMENT USED
_____
_____

RESULTS
_____
_____

DISEASE
☐ YES   ☐ NO

TREATMENT USED
_____
_____

RESULTS
_____
_____

RATING
☆☆☆☆☆

SOWN FROM SEED

DATE SOWN _____	DAYS TO BLOOM/HARVEST _____
DATE GERMINATED _____	DATE BLOOMED /HARVESTED _____
DATE PLANTED OUT _____	TOTAL BLOOMS/HARVEST _____

TRANSPLANTED

DATE PLANTED _____	DATE BLOOMED/ HARVESTED _____
DATE OF FIRST BUD _____	TOTAL BLOOMS/HARVEST _____
DATE(S) OF PRUNING _____	DATE SPLIT/ TRANSPLANTED _____

IMPORTANT EVENTS/CHANGES
_____
_____
_____
_____
_____
_____

NOTES
_____
_____
_____
_____
_____

PLANT DESCRIPTION

☐ #_____ NAME _____ SUPPLIER #S _____ PRICE _____

LIGHT REQUIREMENTS	WATERING REQUIREMENTS	ZONE HARDINESS	NEED TO OVERWINTER?
☼ ☐ ☀ ☐ ● ☐	◊ ◊◊ ◊◊◊	_____	☐ YES ☐ NO DATE _____

NEW-TO-ME PLANT?   QTY   TYPE   ☐ FLOWER   ☐ FRUIT   ☐ VEGETABLE   ☐ HERB

☐ YES ☐ NO   _____ ☐ SHRUB ☐ TREE ☐ OTHER: _____

LIFE CYCLE   ☐ ANNUAL ☐ BIENNIAL ☐ PERENNIAL

SOWN FROM SEED

DATE SOWN _____

DATE GERMINATED _____

DATE PLANTED OUT _____

DAYS TO BLOOM/HARVEST _____

DATE BLOOMED /HARVESTED _____

TOTAL BLOOMS/HARVEST _____

TRANSPLANTED

DATE PLANTED _____

DATE OF FIRST BUD _____

DATE(S) OF PRUNING _____

DATE BLOOMED/ HARVESTED _____

TOTAL BLOOMS/HARVEST _____

DATE SPLIT/ TRANSPLANTED _____

IMPORTANT EVENTS/CHANGES

_____

_____

_____

_____

_____

NOTES

_____

_____

_____

_____

_____

_____

GARDEN LOCATION(S)

_____

_____

MATURE SIZE

_____ _____
HEIGHT   WIDTH

PRUNING REQUIRED?

☐ YES   ☐ NO

PRUNING RATE

RARELY / SEASONALLY / REGULARLY

PESTS

☐ YES   ☐ NO

TREATMENT USED

_____

RESULTS

_____

DISEASE

☐ YES   ☐ NO

TREATMENT USED

_____

RESULTS

_____

RATING

☆☆☆☆☆ 83

PLANT DESCRIPTION

🌱 #_____ **NAME** _____ **SUPPLIER #S** _____ **PRICE** _____

LIGHT REQUIREMENTS	WATERING REQUIREMENTS	ZONE HARDINESS	NEED TO OVERWINTER?
☼ ☐ ☀ ☐ ☀ ☐	🌢 🌢🌢 🌢🌢🌢 _____		☐ YES ☐ NO DATE _____

NEW-TO-ME PLANT?   **QTY**   **TYPE**   ☐ FLOWER   ☐ FRUIT   ☐ VEGETABLE   ☐ HERB

☐ YES ☐ NO   _____   ☐ SHRUB   ☐ TREE   ☐ OTHER: _____

LIFE CYCLE   ☐ ANNUAL   ☐ BIENNIAL   ☐ PERENNIAL

GARDEN LOCATION(S)
_____

_____

MATURE SIZE

_____   _____
HEIGHT   WIDTH

PRUNING REQUIRED?
☐ YES   ☐ NO

PRUNING RATE
RARELY / SEASONALLY / REGULARLY

PESTS
☐ YES   ☐ NO

TREATMENT USED

_____

_____

RESULTS

_____

_____

DISEASE
☐ YES   ☐ NO

TREATMENT USED

_____

_____

RESULTS

_____

_____

SOWN FROM SEED

DATE SOWN	DAYS TO BLOOM/HARVEST
DATE GERMINATED	DATE BLOOMED /HARVESTED
DATE PLANTED OUT	TOTAL BLOOMS/HARVEST

TRANSPLANTED

DATE PLANTED	DATE BLOOMED/ HARVESTED
DATE OF FIRST BUD	TOTAL BLOOMS/HARVEST
DATE(S) OF PRUNING	DATE SPLIT/ TRANSPLANTED

IMPORTANT EVENTS/CHANGES

_____

_____

_____

_____

_____

NOTES

_____

_____

_____

_____

_____

RATING
84   ☆☆☆☆☆

PLANT DESCRIPTION

🌱 #_____ NAME _____ SUPPLIER #S _____ PRICE _____

LIGHT REQUIREMENTS	WATERING REQUIREMENTS	ZONE HARDINESS	NEED TO OVERWINTER?
☼ ☐ ☀ ☐ ☀ ☐	◊ ◊◊ ◊◊◊ _____		☐ YES ☐ NO DATE _____

NEW-TO-ME PLANT?   QTY   TYPE   ☐ FLOWER   ☐ FRUIT   ☐ VEGETABLE   ☐ HERB
                                ☐ SHRUB   ☐ TREE   ☐ OTHER: _____
☐ YES ☐ NO   _____   LIFE CYCLE   ☐ ANNUAL   ☐ BIENNIAL   ☐ PERENNIAL

SOWN FROM SEED

DATE SOWN _____   DAYS TO BLOOM/HARVEST _____

DATE GERMINATED _____   DATE BLOOMED /HARVESTED _____

DATE PLANTED OUT _____   TOTAL BLOOMS/HARVEST _____

TRANSPLANTED

DATE PLANTED _____   DATE BLOOMED/ HARVESTED _____

DATE OF FIRST BUD _____   TOTAL BLOOMS/HARVEST _____

DATE(S) OF PRUNING _____   DATE SPLIT/ TRANSPLANTED _____

IMPORTANT EVENTS/CHANGES

_____
_____
_____
_____
_____

NOTES

_____
_____
_____
_____
_____

GARDEN LOCATION(S)

_____

MATURE SIZE

_____   _____
HEIGHT   WIDTH

PRUNING REQUIRED?

☐ YES   ☐ NO

PRUNING RATE

RARELY / SEASONALLY / REGULARLY

PESTS

☐ YES   ☐ NO

TREATMENT USED

_____

RESULTS

_____

DISEASE

☐ YES   ☐ NO

TREATMENT USED

_____

RESULTS

_____

RATING

☆☆☆☆☆   85

PLANT DESCRIPTION

🌱 #_____ NAME _____ SUPPLIER #S _____ PRICE _____

LIGHT REQUIREMENTS	WATERING REQUIREMENTS	ZONE HARDINESS	NEED TO OVERWINTER?
☼ ☐ ✹ ☐ ☀ ☐	◊ ◊◊ ◊◊◊ _____		☐ YES ☐ NO DATE

NEW-TO-ME PLANT? **QTY** **TYPE**
☐ YES ☐ NO _____

☐ FLOWER ☐ FRUIT ☐ VEGETABLE ☐ HERB
☐ SHRUB ☐ TREE ☐ OTHER: _____

LIFE CYCLE ☐ ANNUAL ☐ BIENNIAL ☐ PERENNIAL

GARDEN LOCATION(S)
_____
_____

MATURE SIZE
_____ _____
HEIGHT WIDTH

PRUNING REQUIRED?
☐ YES ☐ NO

PRUNING RATE
RARELY / SEASONALLY / REGULARLY

PESTS
☐ YES ☐ NO

TREATMENT USED
_____
_____

RESULTS
_____
_____

DISEASE
☐ YES ☐ NO

TREATMENT USED
_____
_____

RESULTS
_____
_____

RATING
☆☆☆☆☆

SOWN FROM SEED

DATE SOWN _____	DAYS TO BLOOM/HARVEST _____
DATE GERMINATED _____	DATE BLOOMED /HARVESTED _____
DATE PLANTED OUT _____	TOTAL BLOOMS/HARVEST _____

TRANSPLANTED

DATE PLANTED _____	DATE BLOOMED/ HARVESTED _____
DATE OF FIRST BUD _____	TOTAL BLOOMS/HARVEST _____
DATE(S) OF PRUNING _____	DATE SPLIT/ TRANSPLANTED _____

IMPORTANT EVENTS/CHANGES
_____
_____
_____
_____
_____
_____

NOTES
_____
_____
_____
_____
_____
_____

PLANT DESCRIPTION

☐ # _____ NAME _____ SUPPLIER #S _____ PRICE _____

LIGHT REQUIREMENTS	WATERING REQUIREMENTS	ZONE HARDINESS	NEED TO OVERWINTER?
☀ ☐ ✹ ☐ ● ☐	◌ ◌◌ ◌◌◌ _____		☐ YES ☐ NO DATE _____

NEW-TO-ME PLANT?   QTY   TYPE   ☐ FLOWER   ☐ FRUIT   ☐ VEGETABLE   ☐ HERB

☐ YES ☐ NO   _____   ☐ SHRUB   ☐ TREE   ☐ OTHER: _____

LIFE CYCLE   ☐ ANNUAL   ☐ BIENNIAL   ☐ PERENNIAL

SOWN FROM SEED

DATE SOWN _____

DATE GERMINATED _____

DATE PLANTED OUT _____

DAYS TO BLOOM/HARVEST _____

DATE BLOOMED /HARVESTED _____

TOTAL BLOOMS/HARVEST _____

TRANSPLANTED

DATE PLANTED _____

DATE OF FIRST BUD _____

DATE(S) OF PRUNING _____

DATE BLOOMED/ HARVESTED _____

TOTAL BLOOMS/HARVEST _____

DATE SPLIT/ TRANSPLANTED _____

IMPORTANT EVENTS/CHANGES

_____

_____

_____

_____

_____

NOTES

_____

_____

_____

_____

_____

GARDEN LOCATION(S)

_____

MATURE SIZE

_____

HEIGHT   WIDTH

PRUNING REQUIRED?

☐ YES   ☐ NO

PRUNING RATE

RARELY / SEASONALLY / REGULARLY

PESTS

☐ YES   ☐ NO

TREATMENT USED

_____

RESULTS

_____

DISEASE

☐ YES   ☐ NO

TREATMENT USED

_____

RESULTS

_____

RATING

☆☆☆☆☆   87

PLANT DESCRIPTION

	NAME	SUPPLIER #S	PRICE
#	_____	_____	_____

LIGHT REQUIREMENTS ☼ ☐ ☀ ☐ ● ☐   **WATERING REQUIREMENTS** ◊ ◊◊ ◊◊◊ _____   **ZONE HARDINESS**   **NEED TO OVERWINTER?** ☐ YES ☐ NO   DATE _____

NEW-TO-ME PLANT? ☐ YES ☐ NO   **QTY** _____

TYPE ☐ FLOWER ☐ FRUIT ☐ VEGETABLE ☐ HERB ☐ SHRUB ☐ TREE ☐ OTHER: _____

LIFE CYCLE ☐ ANNUAL ☐ BIENNIAL ☐ PERENNIAL

GARDEN LOCATION(S)
_____
_____

MATURE SIZE
_____ _____
HEIGHT   WIDTH

PRUNING REQUIRED?
☐ YES   ☐ NO

PRUNING RATE
RARELY / SEASONALLY / REGULARLY

PESTS
☐ YES   ☐ NO

TREATMENT USED
_____
_____

RESULTS
_____
_____

DISEASE
☐ YES   ☐ NO

TREATMENT USED
_____
_____

RESULTS
_____
_____

RATING
☆☆☆☆☆

SOWN FROM SEED
DATE SOWN _____   DAYS TO BLOOM/HARVEST _____

DATE GERMINATED _____   DATE BLOOMED /HARVESTED _____

DATE PLANTED OUT _____   TOTAL BLOOMS/HARVEST _____

TRANSPLANTED
DATE PLANTED _____   DATE BLOOMED/ HARVESTED _____

DATE OF FIRST BUD _____   TOTAL BLOOMS/HARVEST _____

DATE(S) OF PRUNING _____   DATE SPLIT/ TRANSPLANTED _____

IMPORTANT EVENTS/CHANGES
_____
_____
_____
_____
_____
_____

NOTES
_____
_____
_____
_____
_____
_____

PLANT DESCRIPTION

[ ] # _____   NAME _____   SUPPLIER #S _____   PRICE _____

LIGHT REQUIREMENTS   **WATERING REQUIREMENTS**   **ZONE HARDINESS**   **NEED TO OVERWINTER?**

☼ ☐   ☀ ☐   ● ☐   ◊ ◊◊ ◊◊◊   _____   [ ] YES [ ] NO   DATE _____

NEW-TO-ME PLANT?   **QTY**   **TYPE**   [ ] FLOWER   [ ] FRUIT   [ ] VEGETABLE   [ ] HERB

[ ] YES [ ] NO   _____   [ ] SHRUB   [ ] TREE   [ ] OTHER: _____

LIFE CYCLE [ ] ANNUAL [ ] BIENNIAL [ ] PERENNIAL

SOWN FROM SEED

DATE SOWN

DATE GERMINATED

DATE PLANTED OUT

DAYS TO BLOOM/HARVEST

DATE BLOOMED /HARVESTED

TOTAL BLOOMS/HARVEST

TRANSPLANTED

DATE PLANTED

DATE OF FIRST BUD

DATE(S) OF PRUNING

DATE BLOOMED/ HARVESTED

TOTAL BLOOMS/HARVEST

DATE SPLIT/ TRANSPLANTED

IMPORTANT EVENTS/CHANGES

_____
_____
_____
_____
_____

NOTES

_____
_____
_____
_____
_____

GARDEN LOCATION(S)

_____

MATURE SIZE

_____   _____
HEIGHT   WIDTH

PRUNING REQUIRED?

[ ] YES   [ ] NO

PRUNING RATE

RARELY / SEASONALLY / REGULARLY

PESTS

[ ] YES   [ ] NO

TREATMENT USED

_____
_____

RESULTS

_____
_____

DISEASE

[ ] YES   [ ] NO

TREATMENT USED

_____
_____

RESULTS

_____
_____

RATING

☆☆☆☆☆   89

PLANT DESCRIPTION

#_____   **NAME** _____   **SUPPLIER** #S _____   **PRICE** _____

LIGHT REQUIREMENTS
☀ ☐ ☀ ☐ ☀ ☐

WATERING REQUIREMENTS
◌ ◌◌ ◌◌◌

ZONE HARDINESS
_____

NEED TO OVERWINTER?
☐ YES ☐ NO DATE

NEW-TO-ME PLANT?
☐ YES ☐ NO

QTY
_____

TYPE
☐ FLOWER ☐ FRUIT ☐ VEGETABLE ☐ HERB
☐ SHRUB ☐ TREE ☐ OTHER: _____

LIFE CYCLE ☐ ANNUAL ☐ BIENNIAL ☐ PERENNIAL

GARDEN LOCATION(S)
_____
_____

MATURE SIZE
_____   _____
HEIGHT   WIDTH

PRUNING REQUIRED?
☐ YES   ☐ NO

PRUNING RATE
RARELY / SEASONALLY / REGULARLY

PESTS
☐ YES   ☐ NO

TREATMENT USED
_____
_____

RESULTS
_____
_____

DISEASE
☐ YES   ☐ NO

TREATMENT USED
_____
_____

RESULTS
_____
_____

RATING
☆☆☆☆☆

SOWN FROM SEED

DATE SOWN	DAYS TO BLOOM/HARVEST
DATE GERMINATED	DATE BLOOMED /HARVESTED
DATE PLANTED OUT	TOTAL BLOOMS/HARVEST

TRANSPLANTED

DATE PLANTED	DATE BLOOMED/ HARVESTED
DATE OF FIRST BUD	TOTAL BLOOMS/HARVEST
DATE(S) OF PRUNING	DATE SPLIT/ TRANSPLANTED

IMPORTANT EVENTS/CHANGES
_____
_____
_____
_____
_____

NOTES
_____
_____
_____
_____
_____
_____

PLANT DESCRIPTION

☒ #_____ NAME _____ SUPPLIER #S _____ PRICE _____

LIGHT REQUIREMENTS	WATERING REQUIREMENTS	ZONE HARDINESS	NEED TO OVERWINTER?
☼ ☐ ☀ ☐ ☀ ☐	◊ ◊◊ ◊◊◊ _____		☐ YES ☐ NO DATE

NEW-TO-ME PLANT?   **QTY**   **TYPE**

☐ FLOWER   ☐ FRUIT   ☐ VEGETABLE   ☐ HERB
☐ SHRUB   ☐ TREE   ☐ OTHER: _____

☐ YES ☐ NO   _____   **LIFE CYCLE**   ☐ ANNUAL   ☐ BIENNIAL   ☐ PERENNIAL

SOWN FROM SEED

DATE SOWN _____

DAYS TO BLOOM/HARVEST _____

DATE GERMINATED _____

DATE BLOOMED /HARVESTED _____

DATE PLANTED OUT _____

TOTAL BLOOMS/HARVEST _____

TRANSPLANTED

DATE PLANTED _____

DATE BLOOMED/ HARVESTED _____

DATE OF FIRST BUD _____

TOTAL BLOOMS/HARVEST _____

DATE(S) OF PRUNING _____

DATE SPLIT/ TRANSPLANTED _____

IMPORTANT EVENTS/CHANGES

_____
_____
_____
_____
_____

NOTES

_____
_____
_____
_____
_____
_____

GARDEN LOCATION(S)

_____
_____

MATURE SIZE

_____   _____
HEIGHT   WIDTH

PRUNING REQUIRED?

☐ YES   ☐ NO

PRUNING RATE

RARELY / SEASONALLY / REGULARLY

PESTS

☐ YES   ☐ NO

TREATMENT USED
_____
_____

RESULTS
_____
_____

DISEASE

☐ YES   ☐ NO

TREATMENT USED
_____
_____

RESULTS
_____
_____

RATING

☆☆☆☆☆   91

PLANT DESCRIPTION

#_____ NAME _____   SUPPLIER #S _____   PRICE _____

LIGHT REQUIREMENTS	WATERING REQUIREMENTS	ZONE HARDINESS	NEED TO OVERWINTER?
☼ ☐ ☀ ☐ ● ☐	◊ ◊◊ ◊◊◊ _____		☐ YES ☐ NO DATE _____

NEW-TO-ME PLANT?   QTY   TYPE   ☐ FLOWER   ☐ FRUIT   ☐ VEGETABLE   ☐ HERB

☐ YES ☐ NO   _____   ☐ SHRUB   ☐ TREE   ☐ OTHER: _____

LIFE CYCLE   ☐ ANNUAL   ☐ BIENNIAL   ☐ PERENNIAL

GARDEN LOCATION(S)
_____
_____

MATURE SIZE
_____
HEIGHT   WIDTH

PRUNING REQUIRED?
☐ YES   ☐ NO

PRUNING RATE
RARELY / SEASONALLY / REGULARLY

PESTS
☐ YES   ☐ NO

TREATMENT USED
_____
_____

RESULTS
_____
_____

DISEASE
☐ YES   ☐ NO

TREATMENT USED
_____
_____

RESULTS
_____
_____

RATING
☆☆☆☆☆

SOWN FROM SEED
DATE SOWN _____	DAYS TO BLOOM/HARVEST _____
DATE GERMINATED _____	DATE BLOOMED /HARVESTED _____
DATE PLANTED OUT _____	TOTAL BLOOMS/HARVEST _____

TRANSPLANTED
DATE PLANTED _____	DATE BLOOMED/ HARVESTED _____
DATE OF FIRST BUD _____	TOTAL BLOOMS/HARVEST _____
DATE(S) OF PRUNING _____	DATE SPLIT/ TRANSPLANTED _____

IMPORTANT EVENTS/CHANGES
_____
_____
_____
_____
_____

NOTES
_____
_____
_____
_____
_____
_____

PLANT DESCRIPTION

🌱 #_____ NAME _____   SUPPLIER #S _____   PRICE _____

LIGHT REQUIREMENTS	WATERING REQUIREMENTS	ZONE HARDINESS	NEED TO OVERWINTER?
☼ ☐ ☀ ☐ ☀ ☐	◌ ◌◌ ◌◌◌ _____		☐ YES ☐ NO DATE _____

NEW-TO-ME PLANT?   QTY   TYPE   ☐ FLOWER   ☐ FRUIT   ☐ VEGETABLE   ☐ HERB
☐ YES ☐ NO   _____   ☐ SHRUB   ☐ TREE   ☐ OTHER: _____
LIFE CYCLE   ☐ ANNUAL   ☐ BIENNIAL   ☐ PERENNIAL

SOWN FROM SEED

DATE SOWN _____

DATE GERMINATED _____

DATE PLANTED OUT _____

DAYS TO BLOOM/HARVEST _____

DATE BLOOMED /HARVESTED _____

TOTAL BLOOMS/HARVEST _____

TRANSPLANTED

DATE PLANTED _____

DATE OF FIRST BUD _____

DATE(S) OF PRUNING _____

DATE BLOOMED/ HARVESTED _____

TOTAL BLOOMS/HARVEST _____

DATE SPLIT/ TRANSPLANTED _____

IMPORTANT EVENTS/CHANGES

_____

_____

_____

_____

NOTES

_____

_____

_____

_____

_____

GARDEN LOCATION(S)

_____

_____

MATURE SIZE

_____
HEIGHT   WIDTH

PRUNING REQUIRED?
☐ YES   ☐ NO

PRUNING RATE
RARELY / SEASONALLY / REGULARLY

PESTS
☐ YES   ☐ NO

TREATMENT USED

_____

RESULTS

_____

DISEASE
☐ YES   ☐ NO

TREATMENT USED

_____

RESULTS

_____

RATING
☆☆☆☆☆   93

PLANT DESCRIPTION

_____ NAME _____ SUPPLIER #S _____ PRICE _____

LIGHT REQUIREMENTS	WATERING REQUIREMENTS	ZONE HARDINESS	NEED TO OVERWINTER?
☼ ☐ ☀ ☐ ● ☐	⬤ ⬤⬤ ⬤⬤⬤ _____		☐ YES ☐ NO DATE

NEW-TO-ME PLANT?   QTY   TYPE   ☐ FLOWER   ☐ FRUIT   ☐ VEGETABLE   ☐ HERB
☐ YES ☐ NO   _____   ☐ SHRUB   ☐ TREE   ☐ OTHER: _____

LIFE CYCLE   ☐ ANNUAL   ☐ BIENNIAL   ☐ PERENNIAL

GARDEN LOCATION(S)
_____
_____

MATURE SIZE
_____
HEIGHT   WIDTH

PRUNING REQUIRED?
☐ YES   ☐ NO

PRUNING RATE
RARELY / SEASONALLY / REGULARLY

PESTS
☐ YES   ☐ NO

TREATMENT USED
_____
_____

RESULTS
_____
_____

DISEASE
☐ YES   ☐ NO

TREATMENT USED
_____
_____

RESULTS
_____
_____

SOWN FROM SEED
DATE SOWN _____	DAYS TO BLOOM/HARVEST _____
DATE GERMINATED _____	DATE BLOOMED /HARVESTED _____
DATE PLANTED OUT _____	TOTAL BLOOMS/HARVEST _____

TRANSPLANTED
DATE PLANTED _____	DATE BLOOMED/ HARVESTED _____
DATE OF FIRST BUD _____	TOTAL BLOOMS/HARVEST _____
DATE(S) OF PRUNING _____	DATE SPLIT/ TRANSPLANTED _____

IMPORTANT EVENTS/CHANGES
_____
_____
_____
_____
_____

NOTES
_____
_____
_____
_____
_____
_____

RATING
☆☆☆☆☆

PLANT DESCRIPTION

#_____ NAME _____ SUPPLIER #S _____ _____ PRICE _____

LIGHT REQUIREMENTS ☼ ☐ ☀ ☐ ☀ ☐   **WATERING REQUIREMENTS** ○ ○○ ○○○   **ZONE HARDINESS** _____   **NEED TO OVERWINTER?** ☐ YES ☐ NO   DATE _____

NEW-TO-ME PLANT? ☐ YES ☐ NO

QTY _____

TYPE ☐ FLOWER ☐ SHRUB   ☐ FRUIT ☐ TREE   ☐ VEGETABLE ☐ OTHER: _____ ☐ HERB

LIFE CYCLE ☐ ANNUAL ☐ BIENNIAL ☐ PERENNIAL

SOWN FROM SEED

DATE SOWN _____

DATE GERMINATED _____

DATE PLANTED OUT _____

DAYS TO BLOOM/HARVEST _____

DATE BLOOMED /HARVESTED _____

TOTAL BLOOMS/HARVEST _____

TRANSPLANTED

DATE PLANTED _____

DATE OF FIRST BUD _____

DATE(S) OF PRUNING _____

DATE BLOOMED/ HARVESTED _____

TOTAL BLOOMS/HARVEST _____

DATE SPLIT/ TRANSPLANTED _____

IMPORTANT EVENTS/CHANGES

_____
_____
_____
_____
_____

NOTES

_____
_____
_____
_____
_____
_____

GARDEN LOCATION(S)
_____

MATURE SIZE
_____
HEIGHT   WIDTH

PRUNING REQUIRED?
☐ YES   ☐ NO

PRUNING RATE
RARELY / SEASONALLY / REGULARLY

PESTS
☐ YES   ☐ NO

TREATMENT USED
_____
_____

RESULTS
_____

DISEASE
☐ YES   ☐ NO

TREATMENT USED
_____
_____

RESULTS
_____

RATING
☆☆☆☆☆   95

PLANT DESCRIPTION

[🌱] #_____   NAME _____   SUPPLIER #S _____   PRICE _____

LIGHT REQUIREMENTS	WATERING REQUIREMENTS	ZONE HARDINESS	NEED TO OVERWINTER?
☼ ☐ 🌤 ☐ ☀ ☐	◌ ◌◌ ◌◌◌ _____		☐ YES ☐ NO DATE _____

NEW-TO-ME PLANT?   QTY   TYPE   ☐ FLOWER ☐ FRUIT ☐ VEGETABLE ☐ HERB
                                   ☐ SHRUB   ☐ TREE   ☐ OTHER: _____
☐ YES ☐ NO   _____   LIFE CYCLE ☐ ANNUAL ☐ BIENNIAL ☐ PERENNIAL

GARDEN LOCATION(S)
_____
_____

MATURE SIZE
_____   _____
HEIGHT   WIDTH

PRUNING REQUIRED?
☐ YES   ☐ NO

PRUNING RATE
RARELY / SEASONALLY / REGULARLY

PESTS
☐ YES   ☐ NO

TREATMENT USED
_____
_____

RESULTS
_____
_____

DISEASE
☐ YES   ☐ NO

TREATMENT USED
_____
_____

RESULTS
_____
_____

RATING
☆☆☆☆☆

SOWN FROM SEED
DATE SOWN _____	DAYS TO BLOOM/HARVEST _____
DATE GERMINATED _____	DATE BLOOMED /HARVESTED _____
DATE PLANTED OUT _____	TOTAL BLOOMS/HARVEST _____

TRANSPLANTED
DATE PLANTED _____	DATE BLOOMED/ HARVESTED _____
DATE OF FIRST BUD _____	TOTAL BLOOMS/HARVEST _____
DATE(S) OF PRUNING _____	DATE SPLIT/ TRANSPLANTED _____

IMPORTANT EVENTS/CHANGES
_____
_____
_____
_____
_____
_____

NOTES
_____
_____
_____
_____
_____
_____

PLANT DESCRIPTION

☐ # _____ NAME _____ SUPPLIER #S _____ PRICE _____

LIGHT REQUIREMENTS	WATERING REQUIREMENTS	ZONE HARDINESS	NEED TO OVERWINTER?
☼ ☐ ☀ ☐ ☀ ☐	◊ ◊◊ ◊◊◊	_____	☐ YES ☐ NO DATE _____

NEW-TO-ME PLANT? QTY TYPE ☐ FLOWER ☐ FRUIT ☐ VEGETABLE ☐ HERB
☐ YES ☐ NO _____ ☐ SHRUB ☐ TREE ☐ OTHER: _____
LIFE CYCLE ☐ ANNUAL ☐ BIENNIAL ☐ PERENNIAL

SOWN FROM SEED

DATE SOWN _____

DAYS TO BLOOM/HARVEST _____

DATE GERMINATED _____

DATE BLOOMED /HARVESTED _____

DATE PLANTED OUT _____

TOTAL BLOOMS/HARVEST _____

TRANSPLANTED

DATE PLANTED _____

DATE BLOOMED/ HARVESTED _____

DATE OF FIRST BUD _____

TOTAL BLOOMS/HARVEST _____

DATE(S) OF PRUNING _____

DATE SPLIT/ TRANSPLANTED _____

IMPORTANT EVENTS/CHANGES

_____

_____

_____

_____

_____

NOTES

_____

_____

_____

_____

_____

_____

GARDEN LOCATION(S)

_____

MATURE SIZE

_____ _____
HEIGHT   WIDTH

PRUNING REQUIRED?

☐ YES   ☐ NO

PRUNING RATE

RARELY / SEASONALLY / REGULARLY

PESTS

☐ YES   ☐ NO

TREATMENT USED

_____

RESULTS

_____

DISEASE

☐ YES   ☐ NO

TREATMENT USED

_____

RESULTS

_____

RATING

☆☆☆☆☆ 97

PLANT DESCRIPTION

_____ **NAME** _____ **SUPPLIER #S** _____ **PRICE** _____

LIGHT REQUIREMENTS	WATERING REQUIREMENTS	ZONE HARDINESS	NEED TO OVERWINTER?
☼ ☐ ✹ ☐ ☀ ☐	◊ ◊◊ ◊◊◊ _____		☐ YES ☐ NO DATE

NEW-TO-ME PLANT? **QTY** **TYPE**
☐ YES ☐ NO _____

☐ FLOWER ☐ FRUIT ☐ VEGETABLE ☐ HERB
☐ SHRUB ☐ TREE ☐ OTHER: _____

LIFE CYCLE ☐ ANNUAL ☐ BIENNIAL ☐ PERENNIAL

GARDEN LOCATION(S)
_____
_____

MATURE SIZE
_____ _____
HEIGHT   WIDTH

PRUNING REQUIRED?
☐ YES   ☐ NO

PRUNING RATE
RARELY / SEASONALLY / REGULARLY

PESTS
☐ YES   ☐ NO

TREATMENT USED
_____
_____

RESULTS
_____
_____

DISEASE
☐ YES   ☐ NO

TREATMENT USED
_____
_____

RESULTS
_____
_____

SOWN FROM SEED

DATE SOWN	DAYS TO BLOOM/HARVEST
DATE GERMINATED	DATE BLOOMED /HARVESTED
DATE PLANTED OUT	TOTAL BLOOMS/HARVEST

TRANSPLANTED

DATE PLANTED	DATE BLOOMED/ HARVESTED
DATE OF FIRST BUD	TOTAL BLOOMS/HARVEST
DATE(S) OF PRUNING	DATE SPLIT/ TRANSPLANTED

IMPORTANT EVENTS/CHANGES
_____
_____
_____
_____
_____

NOTES
_____
_____
_____
_____
_____

RATING
☆☆☆☆☆

PLANT DESCRIPTION

_____ NAME _____ SUPPLIER #S _____ PRICE _____

LIGHT REQUIREMENTS ☼ ☐ ☀ ☐ ● ☐   WATERING REQUIREMENTS ◊ ◊◊ ◊◊◊   ZONE HARDINESS _____   NEED TO OVERWINTER? ☐ YES ☐ NO   DATE _____

NEW-TO-ME PLANT? ☐ YES ☐ NO   QTY _____   TYPE   ☐ FLOWER ☐ FRUIT ☐ VEGETABLE ☐ HERB
☐ SHRUB ☐ TREE ☐ OTHER: _____
LIFE CYCLE ☐ ANNUAL ☐ BIENNIAL ☐ PERENNIAL

SOWN FROM SEED

DATE SOWN _____   DAYS TO BLOOM/HARVEST _____

DATE GERMINATED _____   DATE BLOOMED /HARVESTED _____

DATE PLANTED OUT _____   TOTAL BLOOMS/HARVEST _____

TRANSPLANTED

DATE PLANTED _____   DATE BLOOMED/ HARVESTED _____

DATE OF FIRST BUD _____   TOTAL BLOOMS/HARVEST _____

DATE(S) OF PRUNING _____   DATE SPLIT/ TRANSPLANTED _____

IMPORTANT EVENTS/CHANGES

_____
_____
_____
_____
_____

NOTES

_____
_____
_____
_____
_____

GARDEN LOCATION(S)

_____

MATURE SIZE

_____
HEIGHT   WIDTH

PRUNING REQUIRED?
☐ YES   ☐ NO

PRUNING RATE
RARELY / SEASONALLY / REGULARLY

PESTS
☐ YES   ☐ NO
TREATMENT USED
_____
_____
RESULTS
_____
_____

DISEASE
☐ YES   ☐ NO
TREATMENT USED
_____
_____
RESULTS
_____
_____

RATING
☆☆☆☆☆ 99

NOTES

NOTES

NOTES

NOTES

NOTES

NOTES

NOTES

NOTES

NOTES

NOTES

www.ingramcontent.com/pod-product-compliance
Lightning Source LLC
Chambersburg PA
CBHW061754020426
42331CB00006B/1476